The Transmission of the Mind
Outside the Teaching

VOLUME ONE
The first volume of a new series

The Transmission
of the Mind
Outside the Teaching

UPĀSAKA LU K'UAN YÜ
(Charles Luk)

RIDER & COMPANY
LONDON

Rider and Company
3 Fitzroy Square London W1

An Imprint of the Hutchinson Publishing Group

London Melbourne Sydney Auckland
Wellington Johannesburg Cape Town
and agencies throughout the world

First published 1974
© Lu K'uan Yü 1974

This book is set in Monophoto Bembo by
Oliver Burridge Filmsetting Ltd, Crawley, Sussex,
printed in Great Britain by Anchor Press
and bound by Wm. Brendon,
both of Tiptree, Essex.

ISBN 0 09 119280 3 (cased)
0 09 119281 1 (paperback)

Respectfully dedicated to the Venerable Upāsaka Denis McCauley whose encouragement has sustained my humble efforts to present to Western Buddhists the Mind Dharma as taught in my country.

Contents

Preface

We take refuge in the Buddha,
We take refuge in the Dharma,
We take refuge in the Saṅgha,
We take refuge in the Triple Gem within ourselves.

OUR presentation of Mahāyāna and Ch'an texts has always envolved the three essentials, namely theory, practice and realization so that the average reader can, without a teacher, study the teaching, undergo the relevant training and realize the same goal achieved by the great masters in China.

Along the same line, we now present the first of ten volumes of *The Transmission of the Mind outside the teaching*, a translation of the Chinese collection of Ch'an texts called *Ku Tsun Su Yu Lu*, each volume being self-contained so that the reader can purchase any one volume if he has no time to read the whole collection. At our advanced age, we do not even know if we can translate and publish all the ten volumes.

The collection *Ku Tsun Su Yu Lu* is a compilation of Ch'an sayings and dialogues gathered by a number of disciples of each master during their stay at his monastery where they received his instructions and underwent successful training under his personal supervision. On their return to their original places scattered over the country, wooden blocks were carved to print their recordings. Due to transportation difficulty at the time, their printed records were accessible only at the monasteries of the returning monks and in surrounding districts. It was not until the Hsien Ch'un reign of the Sung dynasty (1265-1274) that these printed texts were slowly collected from many monasteries and compiled into the present Chinese collection. In our translation, these records of the teaching of each master from different places are separated by asterisks to show that they did not come from one monastery.

The present volume contains biographies and teachings of masters of the first, second, third, fourth, fifth and sixth generations of the Nan Yo lineage of Dharma descendents of the Sixth Patriarch Hui Neng, with explanations and annotations to make the text clear to the average reader.

Since our conditioned language can express only dualities, relativities and contraries, the ancients devised what upāsaka P'ang Yun called the language of the un-born[1] to deal with the inexpressible and indescribable absolute state of suchness. This language of the uncreate is used by all Ch'an masters when speaking to their disciples in order to awake their latent potentialities which no amount of teaching can reach, and is also a means to convey the living meaning of the text.

When a master speaks to his disciples or receives people coming for instruction, he never loses a chance to teach the Mind Dharma. This volume is full of examples set by ancient masters who are indefatigable in leading their students to Bodhi (Enlightenment) by means of the shortcut called 'Direct entry with a sharp chopper'. Each master had his own method of awakening his disciples and readers are urged to read this volume as many times as required to understand the living meaning of the Mind Dharma.

Our explanations and annotations to help readers to understand the living meaning were not permitted by the ancients

1. Cf *Ch'an and Zen Teaching, First Series*, page 76 (Rider, London; Shambala, Berkeley).

whose aim was to leave the students to dig it out by themselves. For this reason the *Bi Yun Lu* or *Emerald Cliff Records* which has been translated into German, was destroyed by Ch'an master Ta Hui on the grounds that explanations by his own master Yuan Wu which were incorporated therein, ran counter to the principle of the Mind Dharma outside the Teaching, which is beyond words and letters. However, the *Bi Yun Lu* was preserved in Japan where it is still available.

In the present Dharma ending age, we are reluctantly compelled to add footnotes without which no publishers in the West will agree to publish our books because they would be unsaleable. We have, however, left some sayings and dialogues without annotations so that readers can interpret them by means of their own intuition, but the best way is to read the footnotes only after they have failed to dig out the living meaning of the text. This kind of exercise will help them to take up the host position while reading or sitting in meditation.

Some of our readers having experienced a major awakening (Chinese, wu; Japanese, satori) we have deemed it necessary to present *The Vimalakirti Nirdesa Sūtra*[2] so that they can follow the Bodhisattva path taught by the Buddha and His contemporary, Upāsaka Vimalakīrti, in order to reach their goal which is Supreme Enlightenment.

In our book *Practical Buddhism* we have related the stories of a European Bhikṣu and an English upāsaka who have experienced a major satori in their initial successes on the Bodhisattva path. After its publication we received the following letter from our English friend about his follow-up experiences:

'It is a long time since I last wrote to you, but each time I open your books we are in communication and I feel a sense of gratitude flow through my being. Now I wish to thank

2. Published by Shambala, Berkeley; distributed in Europe by Routledge and Kegan Paul, Ltd., London.

you for your translation of The Vimalakīrti Sūtra which you have so kindly been posting to me as you completed it. How wondrous it is to read with the eye what the being has experienced; to understand in thought what the intuition knows. The water is delicious and cool as one drinks, but the smile on the face of the drinker is understood. May the gratitude of this drinker be a confirmation to you in your labours that such work carries consequences for the benefit of man that cannot be estimated in mere words.

The warning given by the hermit on P'an Shan to Han Shan when he told of his first experience of dropping his mind and his body in the ocean of non duality, has been constantly with me; do not cling to even this "manifestation of the aggregates". So I shall attempt to do what we both know cannot be done, and in a few words tell you what the situation is from where at this moment I stand.

A year ago I went into a retreat or shessin with a group of young people and for fourteen days we kept up meditation. I passed through the various stages that are now familiar to me, and which I now can understand by reference to your books. One night my body and mind dropped away as happened before; there was the same sense of a burst of light into which the whole cosmos dissolved and with it the incredible sense of bliss. This was the dropping of the ego. But the next phase was different from my previous experience. There was a sense of interweaving of the atoms of the cosmos with the energy that seemed to be the consciousness that was aware of it; this was like being a galaxy that seemed to be dissolving into pure energy that was itself a pulse beat in the total void. At this last point consciousness itself dissolved in Oneness.

How long I remained sitting in meditation I do not know because I was left alone in the room. But the return of consciousness (self-consciousness) was quicker I think than the previous time. There was also the indescribable feeling of weightlessness which I had before which again lasted for a day or so. But the most obvious difference was the feeling that though I could say that I was conscious of myself as being, this sense was no longer located in this or any body. It was as if the whole world was conscious, was a living moving body of energy, which was also at the heart quite still and serene. My mind seemed quite empty of any thought except that it seemed to be able to function; but it was simply reflecting what was around and objective without any subjective choice or selection or attachment. It was certainly like having no head at all.

With this there was a return of the heightened vision that I had before. Everything one looked at seemed not only as if seen that moment for the first time, but also was brighter, more luminous as if glowing. The whole world was radiant. The mind that experienced this was also the thing that was experienced. The complete knowing that is the experience. Not one word can be said that is not one word too much. Oh, my friend, I know why the wise ones of old simply laughed or held up a flower; its all there like the wind through the trees[3] and the sweet cool water when we are hot. Show me your mind and the universe is void.

For a short while I also could see auras of light around those about me. These would change with their moods and thoughts. At times it was as if I was their bodies, felt that I was them and looking out from their eyes. But this soon passed. The light is the darkness and the darkness is the light; consciousness without objects to be conscious of, not even consciousness of consciousness, for there is not even that space for duality to enter.

Reading your books is like meeting old friends. Yesterday I could just understand Chapter 1 and today I can understand Chapter 2. One laughs and says: why of course, how silly of me not to have seen that yesterday. And one day, your work

3. See also page 20 – A gatha on 'The wind in the tree' as experienced by another upāsaka in New Zealand.

13

will be done so well, that even your books will fall apart; but not yet. We shall need them for a long while. They are all in print I am happy to say, and when friends come to me to have dust wiped from their eyes I send them to you. If I had had your help years ago, my inner guru might not have had such a time of it.

Over the years I have received letters from one or two people that you have given my name to. Out of gratitude for the help given to me I have attempted to give them a hint, but they will get all that they need in that direction from your books. To make a start in the great work; to take the first step from reading about it to doing it is the only object lesson really one can give. No one is given anything who has everything already. But if they can't see this; if after reading all the words in all the books, they still think there is some secret being held back from them, what does one do? The grand old man of Ch'an knew when to be kind and when to be tough. In this age I think we all expect things to be too easy.

I have been asked once or twice by young Buddhists if I know of any Ch'an temples where they could go to practise meditation under the old discipline. Are there any still that would either take or be suitable for a westerner do you think? How sad that the great temples of China are now beyond the reach of the pilgrim. Its very strange, but I have always been very attracted to China. When reading about the country or looking at pictures of it I feel it's familiar. Perhaps I came into this life through an eastern gate. Speaking from the point of duality I am sure that I did; but speaking from the 'now' it is a remark without meaning for "I" have always been here.

How strange things turn out. This letter was still in the typewriter unfinished when the post arrived, and with it was your last book *Practical Buddhism* which I had ordered from Rider. It is a surprise to me that you should think my account is worth including as a case of a westerner having this experience. I feel very humble about it though some vanity must be there as I am pleased that you should think it had

14

value. But I would have expected that you would have received quite a number of accounts of the 'wu' experience from people reading your books as I did and then realizing what their experience had meant. Reading again what I wrote to you then, I realize how one tends to try and explain these "cosmic conscious" states in the same words. Its the same experience, or an experience of the same fundamental state; the state of being what we cannot help being, what we are and ever have been, without the million illusions that our age old thinking processes have created. So I suppose as we must use words to "explain" what we are we shall tend to use the same ones each time.

I see you refer to the point that I've also wondered about: if I had known what I have since learnt, would I have become attached to ideas about that experience and either prevented it or perhaps have weakened it by colouring it with expectation? So you also think I might have started Ch'an training in a previous life, relatively speaking that is: as I said above I have always felt that it could have been China. I have over my life had several very vivid dreams in which I was in that country. In one dream I saw the Venerable Hsu Yun as I later saw him in a picture.

As you may guess, I have been reading your new book instead of finishing my letter to you. How glad I am that you have at last got Han Shan's autobiography between hard covers. As you so very kindly sent me a typescript of it some years ago I have of course read it (actually three times) but it will now reach a wider public. Since I first read about Han Shan I found he explained a lot of things that were applicable to my situation. Its quite startling at times how apt he is.

Perhaps it is time to stop all this chatter and show you that I have made a little progress since last I wrote, even if I do spoil it all by rattling on, spilling words all over the page. But first, thank you once again; for your books (and this last one) and all the typescripts you have sent me over the years. Your work has meant a lot to me; the kind of value that cannot be really expressed because it increases with time.'

My friend must have forgotten that in his previous life he had studied the Avataṁsaka Sūtra which teaches the four dharma-realms: 1, the phenomenal realm, with differentiation; 2, the noumenal, with unity; 3, both noumenal and phenomenal are interdependent; and 4, phenomena are also interdependent. This is what master Han Shan referred to as 'the unobstructed interpermeation and intermerging of all things in the Dharmadhātu'.[4] Hence my friend wrote: 'For a short while I also could see auras of light around those about me. These would change with their moods and thoughts. At times it was as if I was their bodies, felt that I was them and looking out from their eyes.' One must pass through this stage before realizing the third of six supernatural powers, or paracittaj-ñāna, that is, the ability to know the minds of other people.

Tibetan yoga also teaches concentration on the palm of a hand until the meditator's eyes seem to fall into that palm from which he gazes back at his own face.

About a year later I received from this English friend another letter reading:

'It must be a year since I last wrote to you, and many times I have felt that I should, but then I think of your work and how busy you must be so that I do not like to intrude on your valuable time. My dear friend, how are you keeping in health? I do trust that all has gone well with you and your work this past year. My thoughts turn often to you for you are one of the few people with whom I know I can communicate at those reaches of experience that lie at the threshold of intuition. One does not meet with such friends often.

I do not think that I thanked you for your last letter, which I now do. In it you asked that I should forgive you for publishing a few passages from my letters without asking my

4. Cf *Practical Buddhism* page 62 The Autobiography of Ch'an master Han Shan (Rider, London; Theosophical Publishing House, Wheaton, USA).

permission. My friend of course you must use anything that I write to you as you see fit; as you say, if the Buddha tells us to sacrifice our bodies, minds, flesh, bones and marrow etc. for the Dharma, what are my few words. Use anything I write to you if it will be of use. It was that I felt that my experience could not really be of interest or value to any one else; but I do realize why you included it now, as it demonstrated that such experiences are not either peculiar to the East or something no longer possible in this sad age of ours.

Do you think that my own account of my search and evolution in the way of the Dharma, if gone into with more details and explanation, could be of help to other Westerners? I hesitate knowing how many very foolish Westerners have rushed into print with their specious advice and doubtful knowledge. Our bookshops are full of such books of so-called wisdom as you know only too well. Or perhaps if I wrote out a more comprehensive account, with the psychological and physical stages I have experienced myself, and then sent it on to you to comment on and use as you saw fit. To ask you this is rather an imposition I know, so I shall quite understand if you write back and tell me you do not wish to be bothered. But you must partly blame yourself, for till you saw that what I have told could have meaning and value in helping to spread the Dharma, I had no thought of it as other than a very personal private experience that could be of no interest to anyone else. Anyway I should be grateful for your advice and would very much want your opinion on anything that I wrote; for without your help and encouragement and explanation, both in your books and in your letters, I should still only half comprehend my own experience. You have my eternal gratitude for that.

There is something else I must thank you for; after taking many months for some reason, the book with photographs of the lovely old temples and monasteries of China at last arrived some months ago. Please forgive me for not writing to thank you at once. I knew I should have written to you months ago. I have sat looking at these pictures and felt that they are vaguely familiar; in particular those that are built on top of the steep mountains and are approached by stone steps. A temple on a steep mountain by the sea; anyway, a mountain with a building on top has always figured in the strange dreams I have had at times which always made me feel they might be memories from some distant past life. Perhaps Mt Putu on an island off Chekiang might be the place; one would have to go there in person and see what came back. Anyway I am very glad to have the book and thank you once again for sending it to me.

In my practice now I am at that stage where after dropping body and mind and being in a state of luminosity where all phenomenal multiplicity is dropped into the still bliss of the One. To stop in this state or to think it is the ultimate I realize is wrong; it is nothing extraordinary in itself though its bliss is very seductive. This is only the joy characteristic of Self as Master Han Shan says. Attainment is instant and complete and all embracing so it is also no attainment and nothing is attained for there has never been any departure from that which is. Practice must follow each in and out breath for the seeds of age old habits are sown deep and the weeding will never end till the Bodhisattvaś vow is realized.

Consciousness is not held in the body when the body is dropped; it reaches to the edge of the Cosmos and is one with the energy that infuses the Galaxies. It is the Tathāgata and nothing else is. This is experienced without discursive thought by instant perception and is a total knowing. With this experience there also go certain physical changes and manifestations; weightlessness, sweating, sometimes the feeling that a force is pushing up the spine from the seat to the top of the head where it will sometimes seem to explode in light with a certain feeling of joy. These I now understand are manifestations of a greater progress in the meditation and as the body is only the union of illusory elements there is no attachment when the mind is still. So there is no attainment

18

and nothing that attains; even pure consciousness must know none other than its one and total oneness or duality again creeps in and mind is in ignorance.'

I hope my friend will give a detailed account of his experiences in a book written by himself for the benefit of all students of the Dharma in the West. As far as I know there is every possibility that he will do this in the not distant future.

From New Zealand I have received the following letter from another upāsaka:

'Thank you for your wonderful books on Ch'an. They have profoundly changed my life.

For some years I meditated on a Tibetan maṇḍala but I was achieving very little success despite great application on my part. Then I came across your books *Ch'an and Zen Teaching* and *The Secrets of Chinese Meditation*. I knew nothing of Ch'an before this, but by reading your books I came to know as much, I suspect, as is possible to know with the intellect about Ch'an, and more importantly I was fired to practise the Ch'an method. I took the kung an "All things are returnable to the One, to where does the One return?" and held it diligently. At first the mind was crowded with thoughts but gradually a change took place until I was able to clear my mind of all but the kung an. Then I could go no further. All seemed lost. I felt useless and lost. But I was determined and I withdrew to solitude in the mountains where I walked and worked until bodily exhausted, all the while keeping the kung an in my mind.

Then one day I stopped by a river and sat exhausted. Suddenly I heard, not with my ears it seemed, the sigh of the wind in the trees. Immediately I passed from my state of exhaustion into one where I was so relaxed I felt open to total flow, over and round and through my body, which was far more than my body. Everything was dripping with white-hot light or electricity (although there were no objects as such) and it was as though I was watching the whole cosmos coming into being, constantly, molten. How can there be so much light?

Layers and layers of light upon light upon light. All is illumination. The dominant impression was that of entering into the very marrow of existence – no forms, no personalities, no deities, just bliss.

I don't know how long I stayed in this state. But when I became aware of my surroundings they seemed different – more alive, not mere objects but rather processes, constantly becoming. I had an overwhelming desire to dance and run and sing and shout but eventually I controlled this and again I was struck by this intense state of illumination and bliss and this time I was able to observe, so to speak, its process and now I am able to recapture this state at will.

When I returned to my hut I wrote this verse, or rather this verse bubbled out from me unbidden:

> The sigh of the wind in the tree
> Contains another wind
> That is sighed by the wind in the tree.
> In the tree the sigh of the wind
> Contains another tree
> That is sighed by the wind in the tree.

I am profoundly grateful that our paths have crossed in this indirect manner, through printed words, because truly it was your books that were the cause of me finding this bliss. Although we have never met and, I fear, never will in this existence, you have been my master and I am deeply grateful.'

It is wonderful that this upāsaka in New Zealand who had never been in China, could remember and revive our Ch'an tradition according to which each ancient master chanted a gāthā after experiencing a major satori!

This upāsaka has forgotten that in his previous life he had studied The Laṅkāvatāra Sūtra from which we quote the relevant paragraph:

'Sitting in the stillness of a mountain or of a grove to pass through the low, medium and high stages of an all-embracing meditation, one will be able to perceive one's own mind from

20

which perverse thoughts flow continuously, thereby winning the praise from Buddhas in countless lands who will confer upon him the sprinkling ordination; realizing the samādhi of comfortable sovereignty and supernatural powers; and finding oneself in the company of kalyāṇamitra (men of good counsel), Bodhisattvas and disciples of the Buddha. As a result one will be disengaged from all phenomena created by perverse thoughts which arise from one's mind, intellect and consciousness, and screen one's nature, and will be liberated from all karmic passions that landed him in the ocean of birth and death. Therefore, Mahāmati, all practisers (of meditation) should always call on men of good counsel who are unsurpassable companions.'

My friend failed in his meditation on a Tibetan maṇḍala because he was not initiated into the Tibetan sect by a competent guru. In the absence of a living guru, he should invoke past gurus of the lineage of the sect (either yellow, red or white) and repeat a mantra as many times as required by that sect.

As he failed to report his follow-up experiences for more than a year after his major satori, I wrote him a letter containing a drawing of two feet walking a tightrope from east to west, that is treading from disturbance to stillness, for self-enlightenment in order to wake up his dormant potentiality.[5] As I received no news from him, I again wrote him, 'I have not heard from you for a kalpa and hope these lines will find you in good health . . .' to which he replied as follows:

'I returned yesterday from a stay in the mountains and found your letter waiting. The reason I have not written for so long is that I have had nothing to report, but the day before yesterday I had another satori, so much deeper than the first that it seems ridiculous to entertain the idea of any similarity

5. The reverse, i.e. walking from west to east, or from stillness to activity, stands for the enlightenment of others, or the salvation work of a Bodhisattva.

between them. I remember describing to you in some detail the first experience, but this later awakening defies any description. But one thing I can tell you about is every saying I have read or heard of the Buddha or the Ch'an masters I perfectly understood, as well as many other truths. In a flash I understood everything and nothing, then individually these truths presented themselves and were understood in a perfectly non-intellectual way. Any attempt at intellectualisation just vanished in its own absurdity. Also I recalled the circumstances of some of the Ch'an masters and in an inkling I lived their lives and knew their understanding.

I wish I could tell you more, but anything I can say misrepresents the experience, which is totally beyond words.

Earlier today I started rereading my books on Zen and everything was so trite and superficial I had to laugh at them - except parts of your books, my friend, where truths are stated without stupid attempts to justify them to the "Western mind." Your books will remain useful for the work ahead.

Since my last letter to you I have begun building a boat in which I will sail the world, spreading the Dharma to all who will listen. It will take some years and all my efforts to build, but I know it will be completed, and I know we two will meet some day. I promised you that our meeting will not require of you the same patience elicited by your . . . caller.[6] When I read your letter I laughed and cried together at such posturing. But posturing is the human way - trying to be something else in a vain attempt to become what we are.

There is so much I wish to tell you but words fail me. Keep in good health and continue your work.'

About a month later I received from this friend another letter reading:

'There are two things I wish to ask you. First, in *Ch'an and Zen Teaching, Second Series* you make mention of the ancient

6. This refers to my encounter with a Western monk in a saffron robe. See page 29.

masters having the ability to predict the future. Is this a normal outcome of the Ch'an training? I ask this because for some time now I have been able to do this. At first it was intriguing, then annoying, but now it is unimportant. Still I would like to know if it is usual. Second, in your last letter you said I "have covered half of the Path". Where does the Path start, or end? Where is half-way? Where is the Path?

Since I last wrote to you I have re-read The Vimalakīrti Nirdeśa Sūtra, this time with receptive mind. Now I know its meaning. When I first read it I was confused . . . but with the right understanding I can see the real meaning. It is like the words of the ancient masters you quote in your Ch'an and Zen Teaching; they have a living and a dead meaning. Even the dead meanings of this sutra have some worth for us in the West, but the living meaning is incomparably more valuable. Also I have read and meditated on the accounts of the teaching of Wen Yen in *Ch'an and Zen Teaching, Second Series*. What understanding I have finds expression best in his teachings, I think. One passage in particular turned me upside down. Wen Yen talks about the Self-nature being as hard to perceive as "to pass through a piece of gauze." It is so true, not because it is that hard, but because the passing through a piece of gauze is the most poetic description of the instant of perception . . .'

In reply I wrote to him as follows:

'You have covered half of the Path because you have reached the inexpressible and indescribable absolute state which is the most difficult thing to attain. This is what my Tibetan guru called the "pu k'o shuo – pu k'o chuo" or the inexpressible and indescribable. If a meditator can describe what he has realized, it is not the absolute, but is still the relative state.

The ability to predict the future is a normal outcome of the Ch'an and Mahāyāna training, and is included in the Ten Powers of a Buddha (daśabala) – see the glossary of *The Vimalakīrti Nirdeśa Sūtra* pages 154–5. All devas and some

23

ghosts and spirits also predict the future. The late Ch'an master Hsu Yun predicted the future and the late Professor Carl Gustav Jung could also do so according to his chief pupil, Dr Marie-Louise von Franz who called on me in Hongkong in 1970. One must acquire all the ten powers before one can be a full-fledged Buddha.

I am glad that you now understand The Vimalakīrti Nirdeśa Sūtra and the teaching of Wen Yen or Yun Men. Yun Men's teaching is too profound for the average student. If you re-read both texts again in say six months or one year you will discover more profound meanings. This is the "beauty" of Ch'an texts which few people appreciate.'

The Ch'an path begins when one leaves the wordly state to enter the stream of Ch'an meditation to wipe out the idea of ego and objects, and ends when one leaps over to the other shore of Bodhi. All this is to teach beginners only, for in reality there is no path in the absolute state.

From England I have received the following two letters from another English upāsaka:

First letter. 'In accordance with your instructions for Ch'an practice I maintained the feeling of doubt walking, sitting, working – in every relative aspect of life – even stooling! Sometimes I would get headaches and my shoulders would gradually rise up; however I kept up the practice. I found your exercise for pre-sleep periods excellent and have succeeded in giving rise to the i ch'ing (doubt) in sleep – a very odd state where I am not asleep or awake. This continued for a few months and one night after practising I drifted off into a dreamless sleep feeling much peace. Suddenly I became aware of my presence in a long luminous room, statues of the ancients lined the walls and the room glowed with unearthly energy, too profound to be a dream as I was completely conscious. I decided that I should not cling to this; I gave rise to the feeling of doubt and within a flash an image of yourself appeared – then before I could think of anything everything seemed to explode in brilliance; there was nothing to be seen, and I do not know where I was, all I know is that I awoke later in the early hours of the morning feeling light and free . . .

Within the same week I accompanied my wife shopping at the local market place and sat in the bustle and noise looking into the hua t'ou and giving rise to the i ch'ing (doubt). I asked "Who is hearing?"; perhaps an hour went by, and then, suddenly I felt very light and I couldn't give rise to a thought – only one deep doubt, everything was in this doubt, nothing was in this doubt, I feel like a stupid man. Since then time has disappeared and lost its meaning, and yet the present is nowhere to be found. Sometimes there is a rushing sound during sleep like ZTTT! and brightness smashes me into a state which is neither awake nor asleep. Prajna is a sharp sword but it is so sharp I cannot find a handle. I frequently experience a rising feeling, but try not to cling to it or reject it. It is accompanied by a noise (in ?) the head which is a noise beyond noise, if being has a sound – it is the sound of being and non being at once. It seems to come from a point neither inside nor outside; I feel I have found the mountain with no peak and have decided to worship there. My wife too has practised Ch'an, in January she rejected the Diamond Cutter of Doubts, but now seeing my results has abandoned likes and dislikes, and has jumped over the cliff to join the dead and rotten bones at the bottom; we are very happy and not because of worldly reasons. Thank you so much for your blessings . . . most Westerners think money is happiness; I have never been financially rich but I consider your books and guidance to be of more value than getting material possessions. Again thank you for your guidance . . .'

Second letter. '. . . . Another experience occurred in my practice. I have jumped from the top of the hundred foot pole.

Before this event, I must have been trying to practise the Dharma of No-Dharma. However, I believe that I gained experimental realization of the Absolute, although it is not correct to say "I". The experience was revealed through the function of a shout, and you clearly illustrated those accounts in your excellent texts of the technique based upon using concurrent causes to awaken a pupil. In this particular case, the shout came from a friend, and I halted as I walked quickly down some stairs. Not only the bodily function stopped, but the mad mind stopped. I do not know where I was. Time and space seemed to disappear, but they were not replaced by the void. I felt great ease after this, and time and space clearly revealed that which is not time and space. I have been very interested in the "Five Ranks", and realize its value as a finger to point out the various stages, and then thrown away to fully embrace the absolute condition. With this in mind, I would be grateful to be introduced to an experienced Ch'an practiser within the "West". A few nails could be left in the barrel, and I would not like to be certain that anything has been achieved. I cannot see the worldly, neither can I see the saintly. There is one substance revealing itself through the function of seeming form . . .'

The barrel above referred to by my English friend, was also used by ancient Ch'an masters to compare our body to a barrel of black lacquer and to urge us to train in order to drop the bottom of the barrel and to empty it of its black contents which stand for ignorance.

There are also Buddhists in Europe, America and elsewhere who have made excellent progress in their meditation and have experienced satoris but since they are modest and have not given us accounts of their spiritual advancement, we are unable to relate their realization in this book. One of them is a former German consul in Hongkong who experienced a satori; he gave a vegetarian dinner to his Chinese Buddhist friends before his transfer to another post in the West. Many are those who experience flashes of dhyana and we would urge them to practise the Ch'an Dharma which will hasten their spiritual awakening because of their excellent background.

A Canadian couple, the late Mr and Mrs Carroll Aikins, who helped us to edit *The Śūraṅgama Sūtra* by offering to purchase 1000 copies for free distribution as a guarantee that our publisher would not lose money on it, also made very good progress in their practice of the Mind Dharma. One day in 1963 they invited me to their hotel for tea and during our conversation I learnt that they used to get up at midnight to practise meditation (they were 75 at the time) and that they succeeded in giving rise to the feeling of doubt and in putting the inner fire into microcosmic orbit. Later they wrote me that they had 'a lot of things' to tell me on their return in 1964 but unfortunately Mrs Kathleen Aikins passed away on the eve of their arrival at Aden in the Red Sea on their way to Hongkong.

Before leaving Hongkong in April 1963 they invited me one afternoon to their hotel to celebrate their golden wedding anniversary at which I was the only guest. Mrs Aikins blew out only one tiny candle and told her husband to blow out the other four which he did before I had the time to tell her to continue blowing. This foretold the exact times of their deaths, the wife in the following year and the husband four years later, which proved that when the mind is pure its functioning predicts future events very accurately.

So their plan to build a vihāra for meditation in Canada and to spread the Dharma there by free distribution of Buddhist books and by holding essay contests with cash prizes every year, and so on, did not materialize.

We regret that because of our advanced age we do not teach Chinese and the Dharma to a few readers who have written that they wished to come to Hongkong to take lessons. It is good to know the Chinese language but our

27

Western friends should know that philology is no substitute for meditation and spiritual training. Although the knowledge of Chinese gives access to the Chinese texts it does not guarantee the understanding of the living meanings of Mahāyāna and Ch'an buddhism which can be grasped only after major satoris have been experienced. The Western Buddhists mentioned earlier who have experienced major satoris, do not know a single Chinese character but their interpretations of Ch'an sayings and dialogues are correct. Moreover, our books contain elaborate explanations and annotations which enable the average reader to practise the teachings presented therein without a teacher.

Since many Chinese characters are ambiguous and are of double meaning, the masters used them when speaking to their disciples in order to test their correct interpretations of the absolute. This is why Ch'an masters enjoined upon their disciples to dig out the living meanings of Ch'an texts and not to interpret their literal or dead meanings. It is only when they know how to take up the 'host' position that they can interpret Ch'an texts correctly, for if they take the 'guest' stand they will understand only the dead meaning. It is only after they have experienced major satoris that they can take up the 'host' position.

For this reason a European scholar reviewing one of my books which is beyond his reach, writes, 'Of the accuracy of Luk's translation I cannot speak, partly because I know little Chinese, and partly because I have understood no more than perhaps five per cent of the contents of this book. But I could not fail to note that the translation reads at times rather strange . . . But to have to read hundreds and hundreds of them (Ch'an dialogues) just by themselves is rather like drinking Worcester sauce neat out of a tumbler . . .'

Later the same reviewer urges a group of Chinese Buddhists in the United States to present a Dharma fit for the *white man*. If so we must ask the Buddha to devise a special Dharma for the white race, another for the yellow race, a third for the black race and a fourth for the brown race.

A Western monk called on me twice in 1971 and at each visit he wrote Chinese characters on a piece of paper probably to impress me with his knowledge of Chinese which he had picked up during his short stay in Thailand. As I spoke of Western Buddhists who had experienced major satoris I inadvertently incurred his displeasure, and during his second visit he urged me to stop my translation work. I told him I could not because I was ordered by the late master Hsu Yun to translate Chinese texts into English for the West, he immediately changed his opinion and said, 'If so you should continue your translations.'

The Buddha Dharma is nobody's monopoly, and in one or two of my previous books, I have urged my readers to cultivate modesty and humility without which they will never understand the Dharma, let alone practise it. Moreover, envy, jealousy, pride, arrogance, insolence, the contempt of others, hostility, racial discrimination and the cult of the ego can only obstruct our quest for Bodhi (Enlightenment). The incident caused by the above monk in saffron robe, reminds me of the French proverb, 'L'habit ne fait pas le moine.'

Some modern pundits who have practised the Mind Dharma, have urged others to use some ancient anecdotes or gāthās, for instance, the ten ox herding pictures, as blue prints for their training without appreciating that only their discriminating minds will come into play and will never lead them to the inexpressible state of absolute suchness which is beyond all dualities, relativities and contraries.

In the East there are also pundits who overtly criticize some sūtras which are beyond their reach. For instance, some claim that the Śūraṅgama Sūtra is a bogus sūtra. Others are definitely against the Diamond Sūtra which, they say, teaches formlessness which cannot be proved whereas they are surrounded by rūpa or form which is visible everywhere.

For this reason when I received a letter from a Western teacher who went to Thailand and wrote me that she would proceed further south in search for Zen masters, I advised her to be very cautious thereby inadvertently incurring her displeasure, for she was full of enthusiasm about the easiness of meeting Zen masters everywhere in the East. She doubted the sincerity of my advice not to waste time and money for no purpose.

I gave her the advice because I have seen Westerners who came to the East where they shaved their heads to join the Saṅgha order and who after staying for some time, got discouraged and disrobed to return to lay life after vilifying the Buddha Dharma which is beyond their reach.

I would urge readers who are intent on studying and spreading the Dharma in the West, to practise kṣānti or patient endurance, so that they can control their minds when they are wrongly criticized, vilified, humiliated and insulted, for the Buddha forbids retaliation under all circumstances. As to the practice of kṣānti readers will find detailed explanation on page 112 note 161.

Upāsaka Lu K'uan Yü

Hongkong

Genealogical Chart of
The Dharma Descendants of the
Sixth Patriarch Hui Neng

The Nan Yo Lineage

First generation   Huai Jang of Nan Yo Mountain
                       (677–744)

Second generation   Ma Tsu (Tao I) of Chiang Hsi (Kiangsi)
                       – Died 788

Third generation   Huai Hai (Ta Chih) of Pai Chang
                       Mountain – Died 814

Fourth generation   Hsi Yun of Huang Po Mountain – Died
                       in Ta Chung reign (847–859)

Fifth generation   I Hsuan of Lin Chi – Died 867 (Already
                       presented in *Ch'an and Zen Teaching,
                       Second Series*. Rider, London; Shambala,
                       Berkeley)

Sixth generation   Hsing Hua – Died in Tung Kuang reign
                       (923–925)

The First Generation After The Patriarch Hui Neng: Ch'an Master Huai Jang

CH'AN master Huai Jang of Nan Yo peak was a native of Chin Chou district (now An K'ang in Shensi province). His lay surname was Tu and his birth took place on the eighth day of the fourth month of the second year of Yi Feng reign (14 May 677).

When he was born the state astrologer saw an auspicious white vapour in the sky and reported the remarkable sign to emperor Kao Tsung. The emperor asked him what this portended and he replied that it augured the birth in the country of an eminent monk who would disregard worldly fame. The monarch then ordered prefect Han Chieh to visit and congratulate the Tu family on the happy occasion.

The Tu family had three sons and the master was the youngest. At the age of three he differed greatly from other children and was noted for his kindness and humility. Hence his father gave him the name of Huai Jang (lit. Harbouring Humility).

When he was ten years old he was interested only in reading Buddhist books. One day the Tripiṭaka-master[1] Hsuan Ching passed before the house and saw the child. Surprised by his unusual features, Hsuan Ching said to his parents,

---

1. Tripiṭaka-master: a monk well-versed in the Tripiṭaka which comprises: sūtras (sermons), śāstras (treatises) and vinaya (the precepts).

'If your child leaves home he will realize the Supreme Vehicle and will liberate many living beings'.

At 15 he left his parents and went to Yu Ch'uan monastery at Ching Chou where he joined the Saṅgha and became a disciple of Vinaya-master[2] Hung Ching. In the second year of T'ung T'ien reign (697) he was ordained and began studying the Vinaya-piṭaka.[3]

One day he said with a sigh, 'Leavers of homes aim at realizing the transcendental (wu wei) Dharma which is unsurpassed in the worlds of devas and men.' The monks at the monastery, struck by his high resolution, urged him to call on Ch'an master Hui An on Sung Shan mountain who initiated him into the Mind Dharma. He then proceeded to Ts'ao Ch'i to pay reverence to the Sixth Patriarch Hui Neng.

Asked by the patriarch where he came from, he replied, 'From the monastery of master Hui An at Sung Shan'. The patriarch asked, 'What thing is it and how does it come?' The master was speechless, and eight years later one day he suddenly experienced some spiritual awakening and said to the patriarch, 'I have experienced some awakening.' The patriarch asked, 'What is it?' The master replied, 'To say it is like something misses the mark.' The patriarch asked, 'Can it still be practised and experienced?' The master replied, 'Although its cultivation and experiencing are not uncalled for, it cannot be sullied.' The patriarch said, 'Just that which cannot be sullied is protected and thought of by all Buddhas. It is so for you and also for me. The Twenty-seventh Indian Patriarch Prajñātāra predicted about you as follows:

Though China is vast there is no other
Path than that trodden by the descendants

2. Vinaya-master: a monk specializing in discipline, one of the three divisions of the Buddhist canon Tripiṭaka, the other two being sūtras and śāstras.

3. Vinaya-piṭaka; the canon of morality and discipline.

Of the Golden Cock who brought in its beak a grain
Of corn to offer to an arhat-monk at Shih Fang.[4]

and about your successor as follows:

On the bank of the Han river is revealed
The subject that is hidden in the mind.
The ripples on the lake seek out the moon in water
Which will illume only two or three disciples.[5]

The patriarch continued, 'My predecessor ordered me to stop transmitting the robe but to hand down the Dharma only. For if the robe is handed down, the life of its possessor will hang by a hair. Therefore, spread the Dharma to convert people'. Now listen to my gāthā:

The Mind-ground holds the (flower) seeds
Which sprout when falls the all-pervading rain.
The wisdom-flower of instantaneous awakening
Cannot fail to bear the Bodhi-fruit.

'After you a colt[6] will rush out, trample on and kill people all over the world. The answer will be found in your mind but do not speak of it too soon.'

The master served the patriarch for fifteen years and in the second year of Hsien T'ien reign (712) he went to Nan Yo peak where he stayed at Po Jo monastery. (The gist of) his instruction ran as follows:

'All things spring from the mind but since the mind creates

4. Golden Cock is Bodhidharma and the grain of corn his Mind Dharma. His descendants are the Chinese patriarchs and masters, Huai Jang included, who spread his teaching.

The arhat-monk is Ma Tsu and Shih Fang his place of birth. (See the following story of Ma Tsu).

5. Han river at Han Chou, the place of birth of Ma Tsu. Ripples stand for strivings in search for the moon or enlightenment.

6. A colt or horse is called 'ma' in Chinese; Ma was also the lay surname of Ma Tsu and Tsu means ancestor or founder (of his school).

nothing, they cannot stay. If you understand the mind you will be free from all obstructions. Be careful to reveal this only to those of high spirituality.'

*

A monk asked the master, 'If a (metal) mirror is melted to make a statue, when the statue is finished, where does the brightness (of the mirror) go?'

The master replied, 'It is like your former appearance before you left home to join the order; where has it gone?'

The monk asked, 'When the statue is finished why does it no longer reflect objects?'

The master replied, 'Although it does not reflect objects, you cannot abuse it in the least.'[7]

*

Ma Tsu stayed in Ch'uan Fa temple at Nan Yo where he had a hut to live in seclusion and practise meditation. He did not look at those calling on him. One day, Huai Jang came to see him but Ma Tsu paid no attention to the visitor. Seeing the unusual expression of Ma Tsu's face, Huai Jang remembered the Sixth Patriarch's prediction and tried his best to convert Ma Tsu (to the Mind Dharma).

Huai Jang then took a brick to the door of the hut and rubbed the brick, but Ma Tsu also paid no attention. After a long while, Ma Tsu asked, 'What are you doing?' Huai Jang replied, 'I am rubbing a brick to make a mirror.' Ma Tsu said, 'How can you make a mirror by rubbing a brick?' The master said, 'If a mirror cannot be made by rubbing a brick, how can one become a Buddha by sitting in meditation?'

Ma Tsu then rose from his seat and asked the master, 'What should one do then?'

7. The metal mirror stands for the worldly mind which reflects or responds to objects or sense data, but the statue or pure mind is disengaged from sense data and does not reflect externals.

The master said, 'If a cart drawn by an ox does not move, is it correct to whip the ox or the cart?' He further asked, 'Do you want to sit in meditation or to be a sitting Buddha? If you want to sit in meditation, meditation is neither sitting nor lying. If you want to be a sitting Buddha, Buddha is not motionlessness; moreover (even its opposite), motion should be neither accepted nor rejected. If you sit (to become a) Buddha, you will simply kill him. If you cling to sitting you will never realize the Dharma.'

Upon hearing these words Ma Tsu awakened (to the teaching), bowed down and asked Huai Jang, 'How should I use my mind to agree with the samādhi beyond form?'

The master replied, 'Your study of the Mind Dharma is like sowing seeds and my expounding of its essentials is like the rain. Since your potentiality agrees with the Dharma, you should perceive the truth.'

Ma Tsu asked, 'Truth is formless, how can it be perceived?'

The master replied, 'The mind Eye can perceive the truth. This also applies to formless samādhi.'

Ma Tsu asked, 'Is the truth subject to creation and destruction?'

The master replied, 'If the truth is perceived as subject to creation and destruction, formation and decay, it is not real. Now listen to my gāthā:

> The Mind-ground holds the (flower) seeds
> Which sprout when moistened by the rain.
> The blossom of samādhi is formless,
> How can it decay or come into being?

Upon hearing these words Ma Tsu awakened to the Mind Dharma. He stayed to serve the master for ten years during which he gradually acquired deeper experiences of the Mind Dharma.

Huai Jang had six disciples whose achievements were sealed by him personally. He said to them, 'Each of you has acquired a special part of my body: one who has won my eyebrows

36

excels in respect-inspiring deportment[8]; one who has won my eyes excels in seeing[9]; one who has won my ears excels in hearing the Dharma[10]; one who has won my nose excels in regulating the breath[11]; one who has won my tongue excels in preaching[12] and one who has won my mind excels in the Tao (truth).'[13]

Later Ma Tsu went to K'ai Yuan monastery in Chiang Hsi (Kiangsi) province where he spread the Mind Dharma.

*

One day Huai Jang asked his disciples, 'Does Ma Tsu expound the Dharma to his community?' As his disciples replied in the affirmative he said, 'I have received no news about it.' He then sent a monk to Ma Tsu after telling him, 'Wait until after Ma Tsu has ascended to the Ch'an hall and ask him this question, "What is it?" Report what he says.'

The monk carried out Huai Jang's instruction and then returned to tell him, 'Ma Tsu said, "For thirty years after my last restless confusion I have been short of neither salt nor sauce".'[14]

The master praised Ma Tsu's understanding.

On the eleventh day of the eighth month of the third year of T'ien Pao's Reign (21 July 744) Huai Jang passed away at Nan Yo. The emperor conferred upon him the posthumous title of 'Ch'an master Ta Hui (Great Wisdom)' and on his stūpa the epithet 'Unsurpassed Wheel' and ordered the vice-president of the Board of Civil Office to compile the master's biography for an inscription on the stūpa.

8. Chang Hao of Nan Yo peak.
9. Chih Ta.
10. T'an Jan.
11. Shen Chao of Ch'ao Chou district.
12. Yen Chun of Ta Ming monastery at Yang Chou.
13. Tao I, also called Ma Tsu of Chiang Hsi (Kiangsi province).
14. Vegetarian food is palatable only if it is prepared with salt and sauce. Likewise life is worthless if one fails to realize the mind for the perception of self-nature and attainment of Buddhahood.

The Second Generation
After The Patriarch Hui Neng:
Ch'an Master Ma Tsu

CH'AN master Ma Tsu, also called Tao I, was a native of Shih Fang in Han Chou district (Szechwan province). His lay surname was Ma and since he had many Dharma successors all over the country he was called Ma Tsu (ancestor Ma).

A monk asked the master, 'How is the Tao practised?'

The master replied, 'Tao is beyond practice. If it is practised and realized, it will decay in the end; this is the way of śrāvakas. If it is not practised, this is the way of worldlings.'

The monk asked, 'What sort of interpretation can reach the Tao?'

The master replied, 'Self-nature is basically complete in us. If one is not hindered by (dualities e.g.) good and evil, one is a practiser of Tao. If one grasps what is good and rejects what is evil, or meditates on the void to enter the state of dhyāna, all this is creativeness (which obstructs the self-nature). Further if (the mind is allowed to) wander outside (in quest of sense data) this is parting with the self-nature to be farther away from it. Just develop a mind beyond the three worlds (of desire, form and beyond form). If a single thought arises it involves the three worlds and becomes the root of birth and death. The absence of (even) a single thought eradicates the root of birth and death and ensures the acquisition of the priceless gem of Dharma-king. From time immemorial because of the worldling's wrong thinking, it unites

38

with fawning, crookedness, depravation, falsehood, self-importance and arrogance to become one whole. Hence the sūtra says that all dharmas (components) unite to form the (human) body which is created when they arise and is destroyed when they end. When they arise they do not announce their rising and when they end they do not announce their death. All preceding, following and in between thoughts do not wait for one another; when they are still and come to an end, this is the samādhi of the ocean symbol,[1] which includes all things like the great sea which gathers waters from hundreds and thousands of different streams and rivers into a single flavoured liquid called sea water, which is a mixture of waters of different flavours from many streams and rivers. So if a man takes a bath in the sea, he actually bathes in all sorts of water. Hence the śrāvaka awakens to delusion and the worldly man deludes himself by keeping from awakening.

But the śrāvaka ignores the holy mind which fundamentally is above and beyond position, cause and effect, rank and class, and because of his wrong thinking he sows causes and reaps effects thereby dwelling in the void for 80 000 and 20 000 aeons.[2] Thus although they seem to be awakened they are really deluded. All Bodhisattvas consider such an incomplete realization to be like a hell for it causes trouble by sinking into (relative) voidness which hinders the perception of Buddha-nature.

As to a man of superior root (spirituality) if he suddenly meets a man of good counsel (kalyāṇamitra) who gives the correct instruction, he will readily understand it and will

1. Ocean symbol: the vastness of the meditation of the Buddha, the vision of all things.

2. Both 80,000 and 20,000 stand for the realm of space and time, 8 for ālaya or the eighth consciousness, 2 for dualities and 0000 for time. This is called the subtle duality of ego and Dharma (relative Nirvāṇa) after all coarse dualities have been wiped out. Cf *Ch'an and Zen Teaching, first series*, 3rd part, The Diamond Cutter of Doubts. (Rider, London; Shambala, Berkeley).

without passing through successive stages, instantly realize his fundamental nature.

Hence the sūtra says, 'Worldly men are reversible but śrāvakas are not.'[3] Delusion is mentioned to reveal enlightenment but since fundamentally there is no delusion, enlightenment is not formulated. For countless aeons all living beings have never been out of Dharma-samādhi (the immutable underlying nature of all things) and have always been taking meals wearing clothing, talking, chatting and using their six sense organs in their daily activities while remaining in that Dharma-samādhi. For their inability to return to the source (i.e. the fundamental nature) they are called seekers of forms and are deceived by their passions thereby creating all sorts of karma. If, in the time of a thought, one of them can turn this thought inward the whole body of his holy mind will manifest.

You all should strive to realize your minds but do not memorize my words, for if you can speak of countless dogmas as many as there are sand grains in the Ganges, your minds will not increase, and if you are unable to speak of them, your minds will not decrease. If you can speak of them those minds are yours, and if you cannot they are equally yours. Even if you can reproduce your bodies *ad infinitum*, emit bright lights and create the eighteen transformations, it is far better for you to give me back my ashes.[4]

3. Cf *The Vimalakīrti Nirdeśa Sūtra*, Chapter VIII, The Buddha path: Mahākāśyapa said, 'The śrāvaka who has cut off all bonds (of transmigration) is no longer interested in the Buddha path. Therefore, the worldly man still reacts favourably to the Buddha path whereas the śrāvaka does not.' (Shambala, Berkeley, USA)

4. When a śrāvaka is about to realize relative nirvāṇa, he can create transformation bodies which radiate and illuminate his surroundings and use his supernatural powers to perform eighteen kinds of transmutation. He aims at eradicating all troubles in the three worlds (of desire, of form and beyond form) by entering the flame samādhi which destroys body and mind to realize relative nirvāṇa.

For he who covers himself with ashes[5] is powerless like the śrāvakas who wrongly sow seeds (cause) to reap fruits (effect, that is to be held in bondage by the idea of cause and effect).

Those who are not covered with ashes are really strong like the Bodhisattvas whose Tao karma is ripe and who are immune from contamination by evils.

If you say the Tathāgata's expedient teaching in the Tripiṭaka cannot be fully expounded in countless aeons as many as sand grains in the Ganges river, this is like an endless chain which cannot be discontinued.

But if you awaken to the holy mind there will no longer be anything of real concern for you. You have stood for so long (in this hall); (go away and) take good care of yourselves.'[6]

*

One day in the Ch'an hall upasaka P'ang Yun[7] asked the master, 'Who is the man who does not take all things as his companions?'

The master replied, 'I will tell you this after you have swallowed all the water in the West River.'

P'ang Yun said, 'Please raise your eyes to look at one who is not blind to his essential body.'

The master looked down and P'ang Yun exclaimed, 'This is a stringless lute which you alone can play so well.'

The text means that it is useless to burn the body to ashes for this can achieve only relative or incomplete nirvāṇa which is still far away from absolute nirvāṇa.

5. This refers to Indian ascetics who cover themselves with ashes, or burn their flesh.

6. These are concluding words at the end of a Ch'an meeting, which mean, 'Take good care of your mind'.

7. P'ang Yun: an enlightened Buddhist of the 7th century. Cf *Ch'an and Zen Teaching, First Series*, pages 74-78. (Rider, London; Shambala, Berkeley).

The master then looked up and P'ang Yun prostrated himself to pay his obeisance to him. Thereat the master returned to the abbot's room.

P'ang Yun said afterwards, 'I just tried to show cleverness which turned out to be stupidity.'[8]

*

One day a monk asked Ma Tsu, 'What is Buddha?'

Ma Tsu replied, 'Mind is Buddha.'

The monk asked, 'Putting aside the four terms of differentiation and the hundred negating terms, will you please point directly to the purpose of the coming from the West.'[9]

Ma Tsu said, 'Today I am not in the mood (to talk); go to the guest house[10] and ask Chih Ts'ang who will tell you.'

8. The above dialogue is very interesting for students of the Transmission of Mind. In order to trap Ma Tsu, P'ang Yun asked him to look up at an enlightened man.

In reply Ma Tsu looked down to reveal the functioning of the enlightened mind. P'ang Yun then praised the master for playing so well on a stringless flute. Thereat Ma Tsu looked up to return functioning to the enlightened mind.

In the second volume of our Ch'an and Zen Teaching series, we have explained the substance (t'i) and function (yung) of an enlightened mind. In Ch'an parlance *looking down* is 'function' which means the mind wandering outside to deliver living beings, and *looking up* is returning function to 'substance' (the mind) after the work of salvation has been done.

P'ang Yun's act of prostrating is 'function' and Ma Tsu's return to the abbot's room means returning function to 'substance' to end the dialogue, for nothing further can be added to reveal substance and function.

9. The four terms of differentiation, i.e. of all things into the existing, non-existing, both and neither. The hundred negative words used in the usual statement that the one mind is neither this nor that, neither long nor short, neither white nor yellow, neither within nor without, etc.

The questioner asked the master not to use the usual four terms of differentiation and hundred negative words in his reply but to point direct to the object of Bodhidharma's coming to China from India.

10. Hsi t'ang or western hall, the living quarters for guest monks from

The monk went to the guest house and asked Chih Ts'ang the same question. In reply Chih Ts'ang pointed his forefinger to his head, saying, 'I have a bad headache today and cannot tell you; go and ask brother Hai.'[11]

The monk went to Huai Hai who said, 'Coming to this I really do not understand.'

The monk then returned to report all this to Ma Tsu who said, 'Ts'ang's head is white, Hai's head is black.'[12]

*

Ma Tsu was gathering rattan canes outside when he saw Shui Liao.[13] Ma Tsu gesticulated as if to sweep away the

---

other monasteries in contrast to tung t'ang or eastern hall, the living quarters for the monks of the community.

11. Brother Hai was Ch'an master Huai Hai, also called Pai Chang.

12. The transmission of Mind handed down by Bodhidharma after his arrival in China is outside the teaching and cannot be explained in words for it deals with the immaterial mind which is indescribable and inexpressible. To explain it in words implies a duality of subject and object and defeats the very purpose of the Transmission.

Ma Tsu instead of describing in words the immaterial mind as formulated by Bodhidharma, said he was not in the mood to talk thus revealing his own mind whose function consisted of uttering these words. In addition, Ma Tsu urged the questioner to call on Chih Ts'ang who would also reveal his own mind in reply to the question.

Chih Ts'ang said he had a headache and would not say anything thus revealing his own mind whose function was to speak these words. Chih Ts'ang urged the questioner to call on Huai Hai (Pai Chang) who would also reveal his own mind in his own way.

Huai Hai said he really did not understand the subject to reveal his own mind whose function was to utter these words.

The monk was stupid and, instead of looking into the three meaningful replies, returned to report them to Ma Tsu who again taught him not to discriminate between Chih Ts'ang and Huai Hai because the mind is neither black nor white and should be looked into to be clear about it for the perception of self-nature and attainment of Buddhahood as taught by Bodhidharma.

13. Shui Liao was a Ch'an master at the time of Ma Tsu. The two words 'Shui liao' also mean a small dirty pool of rain-water on a road.

43

water of a puddle (that obstructed the road) and Shui Liao approached as if to receive the water. With his (right) foot Ma Tsu kicked down Shui Liao who got up to give a loud roar of laughter, saying, 'Countless profound meanings and hundreds and thousands of (states of) samādhi are at the end of a hair; strive to realize their source.'

*

(One day) Ma Tsu ordered a monk to deliver to Master Tao Ch'in at Ching Shan a letter in which he had drawn a circle. Tao Ch'in opened the letter, saw the circle and sent for a pen to add a dot in the middle of the circle.

Later a monk related the story to state-master Hui Chung at Nan Yang who said, 'Master Tao Ch'in was fooled by master Ma Tsu.'

*

One day a monk asked Ma Tsu, 'Why do you say that mind is Buddha?'

Ma Tsu replied, 'To stop a child from crying.'

The monk asked, 'And after the child has stopped crying?'

Ma Tsu replied, 'Neither mind nor Buddha.'

The monk asked, 'If some one who does not belong to these two classes, comes, what will you teach him?'

Ma Tsu replied, 'I will tell him that it is not a thing.'

The monk asked, 'If a man of the right calibre comes, what will you say?'

Ma Tsu replied, 'I will merely tell him to experience the great Tao.'

*

A visitor asked Ma Tsu, 'What was the idea of the coming from the West?'

Ma Tsu asked back, 'What idea is it at this very moment?'

*

Ma Tsu asked a monk, 'Where do you come from?'

The monk replied, 'From Hu Nan (province).'

Ma Tsu asked, 'Is the East lake full of water?'

The monk replied, 'Not yet.'

Ma Tsu said, 'It has been raining for a long time; why is the lake still not full?'[14]

Later, when they heard of the (above) dialogue, master Tao Wu commented, 'Already full'; master Yun Yen said, 'Very deep indeed'; and master Tung Shan asked, 'In which kalpa (aeon) did it decrease?'[15]

The same monk again asked Ma Tsu, 'What is the reason why water which has neither tendons nor bones can carry a ten-thousand-hu boat?'[16]

Ma Tsu asked back, 'Here there is neither water nor boat; why do you speak of tendons and bones?'

*

One evening Chih Ts'ang, Pai Chang and Nan Chuan[17] were accompanying Ma Tsu outside to enjoy the moonlight when Ma Tsu asked them, 'What should we do at this very moment?'

14. Water which can change into ice, sleet, fog, mist, vapour, steam, etc. symbolizes the mind which is also subject to transformation through the six worlds of existence. But despite these transformations, our fundamental nature remains the same for it is changeless.

Ma Tsu wanted to enlighten the visiting monk who, however, was stupid and did not understand the master's good intention. Ma Tsu spoke of the rains that had fallen for a long time, which meant the preaching of the Dharma all over the country; and asked why the monk had not realized his self-nature after hearing the Dharma so frequently.

15. The three masters mean the same thing, that is the self-nature is changeless and therefore is 'already full', is 'always very profound' and 'never decreases in volume'.

16. Hu: a corn measure nominally holding ten pecks but generally holding about five.

17. Three disciples of Ma Tsu who were all enlightened.

Chih Ts'ang (lit. Knowledge-piṭaka or Store of Knowledge) said, 'It is best to (pay reverence and) make offerings to Buddhas.'

Pai Chang (also called Huai Hai, lit. Ocean in the Bosom) said, 'It is best to practise (the Dharma).'

Nan Chuan shook the long sleeve of his robe and went away.[18]

Ma Tsu then declared, 'Sūtras are returnable to the piṭaka and dhyāna to the (vast) ocean but P'u Yuan (another name of Nan Chuan) alone leaps over and beyond all things.'[19]

*

(One day) Ma Tsu asked Pai Chang, 'What Dharma do you teach to others?'

Pai Chang held up a dust-whisk (vertically).

Ma Tsu asked, 'Only this, nothing else?'

Pai Chang threw down the dust-whisk.[20]

*

(One day) a monk asked Ma Tsu, 'What should one do to agree with the Tao?'

Ma Tsu replied, 'I already do not agree with the Tao.'[21]

18. Nan Chuan shook the long sleeve of his robe as a mark of disapproval.

19. Ma Tsu means that Chih Ts'ang still clings to the idea of offerings to the Buddhas as taught in the sūtras and that Pai Chang clings to the practice of meditation the vastness of which is comparable to an ocean. In other words both still cling to names and forms, whereas Nan Chuan wipes out all traces of offering and practice to leap over to the absolute state of enlightenment. Moreover, Nan Chuan's movements agree with the ch'an tradition which consists of showing the function of the mind by shaking the sleeve of his robe and of returning function to substance by going away to retire from the scene.

20. Raising the dust-whisk reveals the mind's function and throwing it down is to return function to the mind's substance.

21. Because if Ma Tsu agrees with the Tao, he will create the duality of subjective self and objective Tao which hinders his realization of enlightenment.

The monk asked, 'What is the idea of the coming from the West?'

Ma Tsu struck the monk (with his staff) and said, 'If I do not beat you, people from all quarters will laugh at me.'

*

(One day) a young errant monk called Tan Yuan returned to the monastery and drew a circle on the ground in front of Ma Tsu, stepped in the circle to prostrate himself before the master and then stood up.

Ma Tsu asked the young monk, 'Do you want to be a Buddha?'

Tan Yuan replied, 'I do not know how to rub the eyes (to see strange things).'

Ma Tsu said, 'I am not as good as you are.'

The monk did not reply.[22]

*

One day a sutra-expounding monk came and asked Ma Tsu, 'What Dharma does the Ch'an sect teach?'

Ma Tsu asked back, 'What Dharma does the Venerable Sir teach?'

The monk replied, 'I have taught sūtras and śāstras at over twenty meetings.'

Ma Tsu asked, 'Are not you a lion then?'[23]

The monk replied, 'I dare not (claim to be)'[24]

Thereat Ma Tsu uttered: 'Hsu, hsu!'

The monk said, 'This is Dharma.'

Ma Tsu asked, 'What Dharma?'

22. The young monk did not reply because he was still inexperienced and did not know how to conclude the dialogue. For instance, he should pay reverence first to reveal his mind's function and then go away to return function of substance. Tan Yuan later became an enlightened Ch'an master.

23. Lion: The Buddha is likened to a lion, in respect of his fearlessness.

24. A very polite term in Chinese, showing the speaker's modesty.

The monk replied, 'The lion coming out of the cave.'

Ma Tsu kept silent and the monk said, 'This also is Dharma.'

Ma Tsu asked, 'What Dharma?'

The monk replied, 'The lion in the cave.'

Ma Tsu asked, 'What is that which neither goes out nor comes in?'[25]

The monk could not reply.

(Later when Pai Chang heard of the dialogue, he commented, 'Do you see it?')[26]

The monk took leave of Ma Tsu and went away. Ma Tsu called him, 'Venerable Sir!' The monk turned his head and Ma Tsu asked, 'What is it?' The monk did not know what to reply and Ma Tsu said, 'What a stupid monk!'[27]

*

(One day) the provincial judge at Hung Chou asked Ma Tsu, 'Is it right or wrong to eat meat and drink wine?'

Ma Tsu replied, 'Eating meat and drinking wine is your allotment of enjoyment; to abstain from both is your lot of blessedness.'

*

Ma Tsu had 139 chief disciples[28] each of them heading a group of devotees in a (different) locality to spread the Mind Dharma all over the country.

On the fifteenth day of the first month of the fourth year of Chen Yuan's (26 February 788) Ma Tsu climbed Shih Men mountain at Chien Ch'ang. While passing through a

25. The Buddha-nature neither comes nor goes.

26. Pai Chang means that the Buddha-nature is immaterial and invisible, but can only be experienced by intuition.

27. Ma Tsu wanted to teach the monk to awaken to that which turned the head but the monk was too stupid to understand the subtlety of mind transmission.

28. Disciples who are allowed to enter the abbot's room for special meetings.

grove he saw a level ditch in a cave and said to his attendant, 'My (old and) worthless body will be buried here next month.' After saying this he and the attendant returned to the monastery.

Some time later Ma Tsu seemed to be indisposed and when the director of the monastery asked him about his health, he said, 'Every day I face the Buddha; every month I face the Buddha.'

On the first day of the second month, Ma Tsu took a bath and passed away while sitting in meditation.

In the reign of Yuan Ho, the emperor conferred upon the master the posthumous title of Ch'an master Ta Chi (Great Serenity) and upon his stūpa the epithet Ta Chuang Yen (Great Majesty).

The Third Generation After The Patriarch Hui Neng: Ch'an Master Pai Chang

CH'AN master Huai Hai, also called Pai Chang[1], was a native of Chang Lo district at Fu Chou (now the Min Hou district of Foochow city, capital of Fukien province). He was Ma Tsu's pupil and attendant.

Every day when a patron sent an offering of food to Ma Tsu, Pai Chang used to lift up the cover of the container and Ma Tsu would take out a slice of bread to show it to the assembly, asking, 'What is it?'[2] This was a daily routine during Pai Chang's three year stay at Ma Tsu's monastery.

One day Pai Chang walked with Ma Tsu down the road when they heard the cries of wild geese in the sky. Ma Tsu asked, 'What is this sound?' Pai Chang replied, 'The cries of wild geese.' A long while later Ma Tsu asked, 'Where have they gone?' Pai Chang replied, 'Flown away.' Ma Tsu turned back and twisted Pai Chang's nose. Pai Chang cried with pain and Ma Tsu said, 'Yet you spoke of flying away.'

On hearing these last few words, Pai Chang awakened (to

1. Huai Hai, the Dharma-successor of Ma Tsu, was also called Pai Chang after the mountain where he stayed at Hung Chou (now Nanchang, capital of Kiangsi province). Pai Chang means: *Pai*, one hundred, and *Chang*, a measure of ten feet, i.e. *One-thousand-foot mountain*.

2. This was Ma Tsu's direct pointing to the mind which caused his hand to show the bread to his disciples and to their minds, the function of which perceived the bread shown.

the mind) and went back to the attendant's hut where he wept bitterly. The monks there asked him, 'Are you thinking of your parents?' Pai Chang replied, 'No'. They asked, 'Have you been scolded by someone?' Pai Chang replied, 'No'. They asked, 'Then why do you weep?' Pai Chang replied, 'The master twisted my nose causing me great pain which led me nowhere.' The monk asked, 'What caused your unresponsiveness?' Pai Chang replied, 'Go and ask the master yourselves.'

They then went to the abbot's room to ask Ma Tsu, 'Will you please tell us the cause of Huai Hai's unresponsiveness that makes him weep so bitterly in his hut?'

Ma Tsu said, 'It is because he awakened (to the Mind Dharma). Go and ask him yourselves.'

The monks returned to the hut and said to Pai Chang, 'The master said you have awakened (to the Mind Dharma) and told us to ask you about it.'

Pai Chang gave a loud roar of laughter and the monks asked him, 'You wept a while ago; why are you laughing now?' Pai Chang said, 'I wept a while ago and am laughing now.'[3] The monks were dumbfounded.

The following day Ma Tsu went up to the Ch'an hall to take his high seat when Pai Chang came forward to roll up the bamboo mat. Thereat Ma Tsu left his (high) seat and was followed by Pai Chang to the abbot's room. Ma Tsu then asked Pai Chang, 'Tell me why did you roll up the mat?' Pai Chang replied, 'Because my nose hurts.' Ma Tsu asked, 'Where have you been?' Pai Chang replied, 'Yesterday I had something to do and could not see you.' Ma Tsu gave a shout and Pai Chang went away.[4]

*

3. This is Pai Chang's direct pointing to the mind which causes these words to be uttered.

4. Ma Tsu gave a shout to show the functioning of his mind and Pai Chang went away to return function to substance to conclude the dialogue.

One day Ma Tsu asked Pai Chang, 'Where do you come from?' Pai Chang replied, 'From behind the mountain,' Ma Tsu asked, 'Did you meet a man on the way?' Pai Chang replied, 'I did not.' Ma Tsu asked, 'Why not?' Pai Chang said, 'If I meet one I will tell you.' Ma Tsu asked, 'Where have you learnt this (good) news?'[5] Pai Chang said, 'This is all my fault.'[6] Ma Tsu said, 'In reality it is my fault.'[7]

Pai Chang then went to the abbot's room for special instruction. (Seeing him) Ma Tsu held the dust-whisk upright and Pai Chang said, 'This is the very functioning which one should keep from.' Ma Tsu then hung the dust-whisk back (on the wall). A long while later, Ma Tsu said, 'In future when you move the two pieces of skin[8] what will you teach your students?'

In reply, Pai Chang reached for the dust-whisk which he held upright. Ma Tsu remarked, 'This is the very functioning which one should keep from.' Pai Chang then hung the dust-whisk back (on the wall). At that Ma Tsu gave a loud shout which deafened Pai Chang for three days.[9]

*

Later Pai Chang went to stay on Ta Hsiung mountain at Hung Chou (now Nanchang in Kiangsi province). His abode was

---

5. A Ch'an technical term which means, 'Where have you learned to realize your mind so that you can perceive all men on the way as unreal and non-existent?'

6. I should not speak of that which is indescribable and inexpressible.

7. Ma Tsu assumed all responsibility because he initiated the dialogue.

8. In Ch'an parlance the two pieces of skin are the lips which one open to teach others.

9. This is known as Ma Tsu's powerful technique of 'ta chi ta yung' or application of great functioning to arouse the pupil's great potentiality, for a weaker technique is not adequate for the purpose.

The deafening of Pai Chang for three days means that he was totally disengaged from the three hindrances, that is sense organs, sense data and consciousnesses. This is the outcome of Ma Tsu's ta chi ta yung which was widely discussed in all Ch'an monasteries throughout China.

on a very lofty peak; hence it was called Pai Chang (lit. One-thousand-foot mountain). In less than a month, people came from the four quarters in great numbers under the leadership of two very well-known monks, Kuei Shan and Huang Po (to receive his instructions).

*

One day Pai Chang said to the assembly, 'The Buddha Dharma is no small question. Formerly the great abbot Ma Tsu gave a shout that deafened me for three days.'

On hearing this Huang Po thrust out his tongue and Pai Chang asked him, 'Do you want later, to become Ma Tsu's Dharma-successor?'

Huang Po replied, 'No, it is only today that I heard through you of Ma Tsu's (technique of) ta chi ta yung but I did not meet him before. If I (blindly) succeeded him as Dharma-successor I would ruin my Dharma descendants.'

Pai Chang said, 'It is true, it is true. If one's views equal those of one's teacher the latter's merits will be reduced by half. If one's views surpass those of one's teacher, one is qualified for his Transmission. You seem to hold views that surpass those of your teacher.'

Thereupon, Huang Po prostrated himself to pay reverence to Pai Chang.

*

A bhikṣu asked the guest monk, 'Let's put aside all questions and answers (in a dialogue); what is it in the absence of questions and answers?'

The guest monk said, 'This is due to the fear of spoiling it.'[10]

When another monk reported the dialogue to Pai Chang the latter said, 'I guessed right about this old brother.'

The monk said, 'Will the Venerable Sir speak (of it).'

10. Questions and answers in the conditioned human language can only screen the mind; hence they are avoided in order not to spoil it.

Pai Chang said, 'No agglomeration can be found.'[11]

*

One day Pai Chang said to the assembly, 'There is a man who never eats but does not say he is hungry; there is also a man who eats every day but never says his stomach is full.'[12]

The assembly did not react to his saying and kept silent.

*

Yun Yen[13] asked Pai Chang, 'Venerable abbot, for whom are you so meticulous the whole day?'

Pai Chang replied, 'Some one needs it.'

Yun Yen asked, 'Why don't you teach him to do it himself?'

Pai Chang replied, 'Because he is deprived of livelihood.'[14]

*

A monk asked Pai Chang, 'I am presenting myself to you with a gem (within me); please throw light on it.'

Pai Chang replied, 'Last night a tiger bit a big worm on the southern hill.'[15]

The monk said, 'No wonder yours is authentic doctrine; but why do not you condescend to teach expediently?'

11. A reference to the Buddha's statement on the non-existing agglomerations of particles of dust that make the world. Cf *Ch'an and Zen Teaching, First Series*, Part III, The Diamond Cutter of Doubts, pages 201/2. (Rider, London; Shambala, Berkeley)

12. This is the state of mind disengaged from sense organs, sense data and consciousness.

13. A well-known Ch'an master.

14. The mind depends on man to purify it for it cannot purify itself.

15. In Ch'an parlance a tiger is called a big worm. Pai Chang likens a tiger biting itself to the monk wanting to know about his own mind, for his act of speaking to the master already reveals the functioning of that mind.

Pai Chang said, 'A fellow who shuts his ears to steal a bell.'[16]

The monk said, 'Without expert evidence it is just as worthless as (cheap) faggot in a cottage.'

Thereat Pai Chang gave the monk a blow of the staff. The monk cried, 'Heaven, Heaven!'

Pai Chang said, 'What a loquacious fellow!'

The monk said, 'It is rare to meet a bosom friend (of your calibre).' He then shook the long sleeves of his robe and went away.

Pai Chang said, 'Today I am half defeated.'[17]

(Commenting on the above dialogue, Ch'an master Fu Chien said, 'In spite of the glorious encounter his two feet were cut off.')

That evening the attendant asked Pai Chang, 'Why did you stop abruptly after that monk had disagreed with you today?'

Pai Chang struck the attendant who cried, 'Heaven, heaven!'

Pai Chang said, 'It is rare to encounter a close friend (who understands you).'

Thereat the attendant prostrated himself to pay reverence to the master who said, 'You have got your pass.'

*

As a weeping monk entered the Ch'an hall, Pai Chang asked, 'What is it?'

The monk replied, 'Both my parents have died, will you please help me choose the date for their burial?'

16. i.e. self-deceit.

17. The monk was correct and in order to test his ability Pai Chang gave him a blow. The monk shouted, 'Heaven, heaven!' to reveal the functioning of his mind. He revealed it once more by shaking the long sleeves of his robe; and then returned function to its substance by going away, that is by leaving the scene to conclude the dialogue.

Pai Chang said, 'To-morrow at the first hour.'

*

A monk asked Pai Chang, 'What is the most wonderful thing?'

Pai Chang replied, 'Sitting alone on the peak of Ta Hsiung mountain.'

The monk paid reverence to the master who hit him (with his staff).

*

The guest monk asked Pai Chang, 'What do you teach to others?'

Pai Chang stretched out his hands at his two sides, closing and opening them.

The monk asked, 'What else?'

Pai Chang pointed a forefinger to his head thrice.[18]

*

In the Ch'an hall the master said to the assembly:

'Spiritual light shines solitarily
Disengaging sense organs from their objects
To reveal the real eternal body
Without the use of words and letters.
The immaculate nature of mind
Fundamentally is ready made.
Just keep from causal discrimination
And you become the Buddha of Suchness.'

*

A monk asked Pai Chang, 'If one interprets the profound sūtras according to their literal meanings one will do a great

18. Pointing the forefinger thrice to the head is to reveal the three bodies of Dharma, Sambhoga and Nirmāṇa of a Buddha which the monk should realize.

injustice to past, present and future Buddhas, but if one keeps from a word of the sūtras one will speak the language of the demon. What then should one do?'

Pai Chang replied, 'To cling to disturbance or stillness is to do a great injustice to past, present and future Buddhas; besides to seek something is tantamount to speaking the language of the demon.'

*

Ma Tsu sent a messenger with a letter and a present of three jars of sauce to Pai Chang. After ordering the assistant to place the three jars in the Ch'an hall he ascended to his high seat, pointed his staff at the jars and said, 'If you can speak correctly I shall not break the jars; if you do not speak correctly I shall break them.'

The audience remained speechless and Pai Chang broke the jars of sauce and returned to the abbot's room.[19]

*

(One day) as soon as the assembly had gathered in the Ch'an hall Pai Chang took his staff to chase the monks away, after which he called out to them. As they turned their heads he asked, 'What is it?'[20]

(Later commenting on Pai Chang's teaching, Kuei Shan asked Yang Shan,[21] 'When Pai Chang called for a second time on Ma Tsu who held up a dust-whisk, what did their dialogue mean?' Yang Shan replied, 'It revealed the powerful

19. The act of breaking the jars is the functioning of the mind and the act of returning to the abbot's room reveals the return of function to the substance of the mind.

20. This is direct pointing to their minds which caused them to turn back their heads.

21. Kuei Shan was the master of Yang Shan. They were co-founders of the Kuei Yang sect, one of the five Ch'an schools in China. Cf *Ch'an and Zen Teaching, Second Series*, pages 57-83. (Rider, London; Shambala, Berkeley).

technique of great potentiality and great functioning (ta chi ta yung).' Kuei Shan asked, 'How many of Ma Tsu's 84 enlightened disciples realized great potentiality and how many great functioning?' Yang Shan replied, 'Pai Chang realized great potentiality and Huang Po great functioning. All the others were just Tao chanting monks (second raters).' Kuei Shan said, 'It is true it is true.')

*

One day Pai Chang went out with the monks to till the land, and when he returned he said to Huang Po, 'It is no easy work.' Huang Po said, 'The whole community worked.' Pai Chang said, 'Sorry to have given you so much trouble.' Huang Po said, 'How dared I shrink from my duty?' Pai Chang asked, 'How many fields have been tilled?' Huang Po gesticulated as if to hoe the ground, Pai Chang gave a shout and Huang Po shut his ears and went away.

*

Pai Chang asked Huang Po, 'Where do you come from?' Huang Po replied, 'From the foot of the mountain where I gathered mushrooms.' Pai Chang said, 'At the foot of the mountain there is a tiger, have you seen it?' Thereat, Huang Po gave a tiger's roar and Pai Chang took a hatchet from his belt as if to chop (the tiger). Huang Po restrained Pai Chang and gave him a slap in the face.

That evening in the Ch'an hall Pai Chang said to the assembly, 'There is a tiger at the foot of the mountain, see it when you go out. This morning I was bitten by it.'

(Later Kuei Shan commenting on the above dialogue, asked Yang Shan, 'What do you think of Huang Po's tale of the tiger?' Yang Shan asked back, 'What do you think of it?' Kuei Shan said, 'At the time Pai Chang could easily have given a blow of the hatchet to finish off (the tiger). Why did he come to such straits?' Yang Shan said, 'It was not so.' Kuei

Shan asked, 'What then do you think of it?' Yang Shan replied, 'He could not only sit on the tiger's head but knew how to seize (and twist) its tail.' Kuei Shan said, 'You understand so well (the situation of someone precariously perched) on a dangerous cliff.'

*

Pai Chang noticed that every day an old man came to the Ch'an hall to listen to the Dharma and then followed the monks when they went away. One day the old man stayed behind and Pai Chang asked him who he was. The man replied, 'I was a head monk on this mountain at the time of Kāśyapa Buddha.[22] (One day) a pupil asked me if a man practising self-cultivation could still become involved in retribution according to the law of causality. I replied, "No, he is free (from the effect of cause and effect)." For this reply alone I got involved in retribution and have been reborn as a wild fox. Will the Venerable Abbot teach me a correct answer to the question (in order to free me from retribution)?' Pai Chang said, 'Ask me the same question (and I will reply to it).' The old man then asked Pai Chang, 'Does a man practising self-cultivation still get involved in retribution according to the law of causality?' Pai Chang replied, 'He is not blind to cause and effect.' Thereupon, the old man was greatly awakened and took leave of Pai Chang, saying, 'I am now liberated from the fox's body. I live on the mountain behind and beg you to grant me the usual rites of cremation for a dead monk.'[23]

Pai Chang ordered the Karmadāna[24] to make a formal

22. Cf *Ch'an and Zen Teaching, Second Series*, The forty Transmission Gathas, page 30 – Kasyapa Buddha. (Rider, London; Shambala, Berkeley).

23. The law of causality ceases to affect a man only after he has realized the absolute state of suchness which is beyond all worldly conditions, but so long as he stays in the realm of illusion, he will suffer from the effects of his errors and mistakes.

24. The duty-distributor, second in command of a monastery.

announcement of the funeral of a deceased bhikṣu to the consternation of the whole community.

That evening, at the Ch'an meeting, as Pai Chang was explaining the cause leading to the funeral during the day, Huang Po asked him, 'An ancient gave a wrong answer to a question and was, as a result, involved in retribution causing him to be reborn in a wild fox's body. What would happen to those giving no wrong answers now?' Pai Chang said, 'Come forward, I will tell you.'[25] Huang Po stepped forward and gave Pai Chang a slap in the face.[26] Pai Chang said, 'This is like speaking of the monk with a red moustache and again of the red-moustached monk.'[27]

*

Kuei Shan was then the verger[28] of the monastery. (One day) the ascetic Szu Ma asked him what he thought of the story of the wild fox. Kuei Shan knocked on the door thrice. Szu Ma said, 'Is it not too coarse?' Kuei Shan said, 'The Buddha Dharma is not that.'[29]

Later Kuei Shan asked Yang Shan what he thought of Huang Po's question (to Pai Chang) about the wild fox and Yang Shan replied, 'Huang Po used to employ this technique

25. These words 'Come forward, I will tell you!' reveal both substance and function.

26. 'Stepping forward' reveals the substance and 'slapping' its function.

27. This is tautology or saying the same things – substance and function in two different ways. The monk with a red moustache was Vibhāṣā, a name for Buddhayaśas who came to China to translate Sanskrit sūtras into Chinese.

28. Verger: a monk with various duties e.g. indicating the order of sitting.

29. Kuei Shan means that it was the story of an ancient abbot who got disengaged from the worldly to achieve spiritual awakening, whose function was revealed by the act of knocking thrice at the door, i.e. full realization of the three bodies of Nirmāṇa, Sambhoga and Dharma, which are above and beyond all dualities e.g. the coarse and the subtle.

(of ta chi ta yung, i.e. greatness in potentiality and greatness in functioning).' Kuei Shan asked, 'Is his technique an inborn one or is it inherited (from a teacher)?' Yang Shan replied, 'It is inherited from a master (i.e. Pai Chang) and it is also due to his correct interpretation of the Transmission).' Kuei Shan said, 'It is so, it is so.'

*

(One day) Huang Po asked Pai Chang, 'What Dharma did the ancients teach to others?' Pai Chang kept silent for a long while and Huang Po said, 'What then will you transmit to your descendants in coming generations?' Pai Chang said, 'I thought you were one of those of large calibre', and then returned to the abbot's room.[30]

*

Pai Chang and Kuei Shan were walking outside when the former asked the latter, 'Do you have fire here?' Kuei Shan replied, 'I have'. Pai Chang asked, 'Where is it?' Kuei Shan picked up a twig, blew (as if to kindle a fire) and handed it to Pai Chang who received it, saying, 'This is like moth-eaten wood.'

*

One day the community went out to work in the fields. When a monk heard the drumbeat, he held up his hoe, laughed heartily and returned to the monastery.

(Seeing this) Pai Chang said, 'What a remarkable thing! This is Avalokiteśvara's Dharma-door to enlightenment.

Afterwards Pai Chang sent for the monk and asked him, 'What have you seen today?' The monk replied, 'I did not

30. In reply to Huang Po's second question, Pai Chang's last words reveal the function of the mind and his return to the abbot's room is returning function to substance.

have any rice gruel this morning and when I heard the drum-beat I returned to take my meal.' Thereat, Pai Chang gave a loud roar of laughter.

*

A monk asked Pai Chang, 'What is Buddha?' Pai Chang asked back, 'What are you?' The monk replied, 'I am so-and-so.' Pai Chang asked, 'Do you know this so-and-so?' The monk said, 'This is already so clear.' Pai Chang held up a dust-whisk and asked the monk, 'Do you see the dust-whisk?' The monk replied, 'I see it.'

Thereat Pai Chang stopped the dialogue.

*

(One day) Pai Chang sent a monk to Chang Ching (another Ch'an master) with these instructions, 'Wait until Chang Ching comes to the Ch'an hall to expound the Dharma; then spread your cotton mat[31] on the ground and prostrate your-self in front of him, then get up, take one of your sandals, clean the dust off it with your long sleeve and turn it over.'

The monk did as he was told and Chang Ching said, 'It is this old monk's fault.'[32]

*

Miscellaneous Records of Pai Chang's Sayings

When you preach, you should see if your listeners are monks or laymen; you should distinguish the difference between general and technical terms; and you should be familiar with the teaching of the whole[33] and partial[34] truths.

31. Niṣīdana, a cloth or mat for sitting on, which a monk carries in a pocket inside his large sleeve.
32. The term 'this old monk' is used for the personal pronoun I.
33. Mahāyāna reveals the whole truth to men of high spirituality.
34. Hīnayāna reveals partial truth to men of low spirituality.

The teaching of the whole truth deals with purity (perfection) and the teaching of the partial truth deals with impurity (imperfection). The teaching on impurity is to pick out the worldly and that on purity is to single out the saintly.

When you expound the nine divisions of the (Buddhist) canon[35] you should know that living beings who are blind (i.e. who are incapable of perceiving the truth) need guidance and training. If you teach worldlings who are deaf (i.e. who are incapable of hearing and understanding the Dharma), you should tell them straight off to leave their homes to keep the precepts, practise meditation and develop wisdom. But if you meet worldly men who are beyond all measure (i.e. who are of exceptionally high spirituality) you should not teach them the above but should do exactly what Vimalakirti[36] and Fu Ta Shih[37] did before.

When expounding the Dharma to ascetic monks (śramaṇa)[38] you should know that they have been fully ordained for the practice of śīla, dhyāna and prajñā; if you again insist on their performance thereof, your talk is inopportune and is also called affected speech.

So if your listeners are ascetic monks you should deal with pollution arising from (basic) purity, and should teach them to keep from dualities such as *is* and *is not*, etc. and from (the concept of) practice and realization as well as from this very idea of so keeping away.

35. I, The sūtra, or the Buddha's sermon; 2, geya, metrical pieces; 3, vyākaraṇa, prophecies; 4, gāthā, chants or poems; 5, udāna, impromptu or unsolicited addresses; 6, ityukta, narratives; 7, jātaka, stories of former lives of the Buddha; 8, vaipulya, expanded sūtras; and 9, adbhuta-dharma, miracles, etc.

36. Cf *The Vimalakīrti Nirdeśa Sūtra* (Shambala, Berkeley; Routledge & Kegan Paul Ltd., London).

37. Cf *Ch'an and Zen Teaching, First Series*, pages 143-145 (Rider, London; Shambala, Berkeley)

38. Śramaṇa are monks who have left their homes and so relinquish all worldly passions.

If these ascetic monks in their strivings to cut off their contaminating habits, fail to wipe out desire and anger, they are also called deaf worldlings. In this case you should also teach them meditation to develop wisdom.

If they are Hīnayāna monks who have succeeded in cutting off desire and anger, but dwell in this freedom from desire which they regard as the right stage, they are (really) in the formless world which screens the Buddha's light; this is (tantamount to) shedding the blood of the Buddha.[39] In such a case, you should also teach them meditation to develop wisdom.

(Thus) you should distinguish between purity and impurity. Impurity has different names such as desire, anger, love, grasping, and so on and purity has various names such as bodhi, nirvāṇa, liberation, and so on.

When looking into purity and impurity, into the worldly and the saintly, into form, sound, smell, taste, touch and dharma and into the mundane and supramundane, you should not have the least desire for or grasp at anything. While in this condition free from desire and grasping, you may think of it as the right one, but it is only the *initial* manifestation of good (roots), a state of controlled mind of the śrāvaka stage which retains the Dharma raft,[40] does not forsake ego and belongs to the small vehicle (Hīnayāna) that realizes only the dhyāna fruit.

If you are free from desire and grasping and do not dwell in this (objective) freedom, this is the *intermediate* manifestation of good (roots) in accord with (the teaching of) partial

39. The fourth of five deadly sins, the other four being parricide, matricide, killing an arhat, and destroying the harmony of the saṅgha.

40. A reference to the Diamond Sūtra in which the Buddha says that even the Dharma should be cast away, like a raft which is abandoned when one reaches the other shore. Cf *Ch'an and Zen Teaching, First Series,* The Diamond Cutter of Doubts, page 167 Note 2. (Rider, London; Shambala, Berkeley).

truth. You will reach the formless world which prevents your fall into Hinayāna and demonic ways, but it is still a dhyāna disease which obstructs your Bodhisattva development (into Buddhahood).

If you do not dwell in this freedom from desire and grasping, and cease to be aware of such non-dwelling, this is the *final* manifestation of good (roots) which is in line with the teaching of the whole truth (Mahāyāna) and prevents your falling into the formless world, contracting the dhyāna disease, slipping into the (objective) Bodhisattva vehicle and the realm of the kings of demons which obstruct prajñā (wisdom), the Bodhisattva stage of development and (the Bodhisattva) lines of conduct, in which case your incapability to perceive your own Buddha-nature is likened to your non-perception of forms (objects) on a dark night.

As to the Buddha stage which cuts off the two refined defilements – the fine and the subtle conceptions of the known – it is attained by a man of great wisdom breaking the veil of delusion and rising above the sūtras. If he passes through the threefold freedom[41] and is no longer comparable to a (captive) deer making three bounds to get out of the net as the teaching school puts it, he is called a Buddha free from all ties, whom nothing can hold in bondage; an enlightened one after (the advent of) Dīpaṁkara Buddha; one of the supreme vehicle and of the highest wisdom who stands erect on the Buddha path. Such a man is a (real) Buddha, possessing the Buddha-nature, a pilot who cannot be moved by the winds of passion, who has won unopposed prajñā; a master of the law of causality, enjoying a full measure of blessedness, wisdom and sovereign freedom, which means his immunity against causes and effects; dwelling in the state of birth which

41. Freedom from desire of the śrāvaka stage, from clinging to this freedom from desire of the pratyeka-buddha stage, and from clinging to the knowledge of such non-abiding of the Bodhisattva stage.

cannot hold him, in the state of death which cannot hinder him, and in the midst of the five aggregates as if standing before a door wide open to clear their obstructions; free to leave and stay and coming and going without difficulty. If he reaches such a state, regardless of its high or low degree of attainment, even appearing in the tiny body of an ant, this is the inconceivable state of the wonderful pure land, but it is still within the province of words used to untie bonds.[42] Since basically he has no wounds, do not wound him.[43] The wounds of Buddhas and Bodhisattvas are (self-inflicted by) their clinging to dualities such as *is* and *is not* and the like.

(This duality of) *is* and *is not* controls all phenomena causing the ten stages of Bodhisattva development (into Buddhahood) to become streams of turbid waters[44], but people (wrongly) regard these stages as standing for purity and so set up purity in contrast with impurity which is considered to be a calamity.

It is said that formerly of the ten chief disciples of the Buddha, Sāriputra and Pūrṇamaitrāyaṇiputra developed the right faith, Ānanda held the wrong belief, and Sunakṣatra and the others set (good) examples and devised rules and regulations. Later they were exposed one by one by their master (the Buddha) for dwelling in stillness for 80,000 kalpas,[45] in

42. Words used to untie bonds are harmful because they set up dualities thereby holding listeners in bondage.

43. Vimalakīrti said to Pūrṇamaitrāyaṇiputra, 'You should know the minds of your listeners and do not take their precious crystal for ordinary glass. If you do not know their propensities, do not teach them Hīnayāna. They have no wounds, so do not hurt them. To those who want to tread the wide path, do not show them narrow tracks. Do not enclose the great sea in the print of an ox's foot; do not liken sunlight to the dim glow of a firefly.' Cf *The Vimalakīrti Nirdeśa Sūtra* (Shambala, Berkeley).

44. They become impurities the moment they are clung to, thereby creating the duality of subjective ego and objective realization.

45. The digit 8 stands for eight consciousnesses that make body and mind i.e. space, and the following 0000 stands for time.

the four dhyāna heavens, in the eight degrees of serenity[46] and in (immortal) arhatship due to their grasping, thereby intoxicating themselves with the brew of (illusory) purity. This is why those who have attained the śrāvaka stage, are no longer willing to develop a mind set on supreme enlightenment.[47] Therefore, those who have cut off the roots of bodhi, are devoid of Buddha-nature. This is what the teaching school calls a dangerous deep pit of (false) liberation which is most dreadful. For a receding mind in the time of a thought will cause you to fall into hell with the speed of a flying arrow. So you should give rise to neither receding nor not-receding, and act like Mañjuśri, Avalokiteśvara and Mahāsthāma who appeared in the śrota-āpanna[48] realm where in spite of all sorts of temptation and enticement, no one could say that they were backsliding as the most that could be said of them was that they dwelt for a short time in the śrota-āpanna stage.

Now in your introspection, if you are not influenced by what *is* and what *is not*, if you pass through the threefold eradication,[49] leap beyond both pleasant and unpleasant situations, and when you hear about hundreds, thousands, tens of thousands and hundreds of thousands of Buddhas appearing in the world as if nothing was heard about them, with also no clinging to the idea of this non-hearing about them, and also without awareness of such non-clinging, you are a man who cannot backslide, who is above and beyond all measure and estimate, who is a true Buddha always staying in the world and who is immune against all worldly pollution. To speak of receding when the Buddha turns the Wheel of

46. Eight degrees of serenity or dhyāna: dhyāna of the four heavens of form and of the four formless heavens.
47. Quote from *The Vimalakīrti Nirdeśa Sūtra* (Shambala, Berkeley).
48. Śrota-āpanna: one who has entered the stream of holy living.
49. See page 65, note 41.

the Law is slandering (the three treasures of) Buddha, Dharma and Saṅgha, and to speak of not-receding when the Buddha does not turn the Wheel of the Law is also defaming (the three treasures of) Buddha, Dharma and Saṅgha.[50]

Hence Seng Chao[51] said, 'The Way of Bodhi is indescribable and immeasurable for its height is unsurpassed, its expanse is boundless, its bottom is soundless and its depth is unfathomable.'

To speak of it is setting up a target for flying arrows to hit. To speak of introspection is not discerning purity from impurity. To say that besides introspection something else exists is demonic talk. To preserve that introspection is also demonic talk and is called heresy.[52] To say that that introspection is self-Buddha is conditioning and measuring (the indescribable and the immeasurable), like a crying jackal (which deceives) and the glue (that sticks and holds you in bondage).

That which basically is neither self-cognizant nor self-conscious is self-Buddha. He who allows his mind to wander outside searching for Buddha, needs men of good counsel[53] who use self-cognizance and self-awareness as a kind of remedy to cure the illness caused by this quest for externals. But when this wandering mind comes to an end, he should, as soon as he recovers from his illness, throw away this medicine. If he clings to this self-cognizance and self-awareness, this is a dhyāna disease exclusively of the śrāvaka stage. It is like water which has frozen into ice and can no longer

50. Receding and non-receding and turning and not turning the Wheel of the Law, are dualities which, if clung to, handicap the manifestation of the Three Treasures of Buddha, Dharma and Sangha.

51. Seng Chao was a disciple of Kumārajīva and author of the well-known treatise Chao Lun.

52. Heresy which denies the law of causality and holds that things happen spontaneously.

53. Kalyāṇamitra, a man of good counsel, or one who is friendly and ready to teach the Dharma to others.

allay thirst; and also like an incurable disease which no worldly physician can heal.

There is not a living being who is not fundamentally a Buddha (but) do not interpret (the objective) Buddha which is used (only) as some sort of medicine to cure the illusion of living beings. When one is cured of this illness, there is no further need of medicine, and the illness should no longer remain.

Clear water is used to illustrate this. Buddha is likened to liquorice or honey mixed with water; the mixture is sweet and delicious. If clear water is not mentioned when speaking of this sweet drink, this does not mean that water is non-existent for fundamentally it exists.

The underlying principle is self-possessed by you all, and the Buddhas and Bodhisattvas are called pearl exhibiters. It is not something (an object) and need not be known or interpreted for it is neither 'it' nor 'not it'. Just cut off the two extremes of the duality, wipe out *what is* and *what is not*, and eradicate the *non-existing* and the *not non-existent* until there are no traces of the two extremes so that you are no longer caught and affected by them; until there is neither deficiency nor sufficiency of them, neither the worldly nor the saintly, neither light nor darkness, neither knowing nor not knowing, and neither bondage nor liberation, for it is beyond names and appellations; if so how can there be no truthfulness? How can there be such nonsense as 'carving and polishing space to produce the form of a Buddha' or 'making space with blue, yellow, red and white colours'?

To preach the Dharma which is without compare suggests a Dharmakāya which is transcendental and is beyond fate and destiny; hence the saintly substance is nameless and inexpressible, like immaterial reality to which there is no analogy.

Like tiny insects which can settle on anything except fire, all living beings can get involved in all sorts of causes except the cause of wisdom (prajñā).

If a man of good counsel is approached in the quest of knowledge and interpretation (of the absolute Dharma), he will give rise to demonic words and speech (which can never reach it). If the Bodhisattva's four universal vows[54] are taken to deliver all living beings before one's realization of Bodhi, this is tying oneself to the inextricable demonic pledge. Pure living, the precepts, meditation and prajñā, are the seeds of morality on the worldly plane, and even if they enable you to sit in a bodhimaṇḍala (holy site) to show your realization of Bodhi for the deliverance of people as countless as sand grains in the Ganges, you actually reach only the stage of a Pratyeka-Buddha due to the underlying demonic seed of desire and clinging. If you are free from all desires and contamination by them thereby achieving spiritual independence and so dwelling in utter serenity without advancing further, this is trifling with the demonic state of stillness.

Even the (so-called objective) supreme nirvāṇa, a state of stillness free from desire, is also a demonic karma, because if wisdom is not freed from some of the nets of māra, even if you interpret (correctly) hundreds of volumes of the four vedas[55] you have only gained hellish dregs, for there is no such thing as searching for something resembling the Buddha.

As to the preaching now usually heard about clinging to neither good nor evil and to neither what *is* nor what *is not*, this is slipping into the void to search for twigs instead of the root, which is falling into (dull) emptiness. To seek Buddhahood and bodhi as well as what *is* and what *is not* is straying from the root in the quest for twigs.

But he who merely eats to keep himself alive, mends his rags to warm his body (in winter), drinks to quench his thirst, and besides these necessaries, completely disregards what *is* and what *is not*, will gradually become clear (about

54. Cf *Ch'an and Zen Teaching, Third Series,* pages 52/3 (Rider, London; Shambala, Berkeley)
55. The four holy Scriptures of Brahmanism.

supreme enlightenment). For a true man of good counsel clings to neither *is* nor *is not*, is free from the ten perverse views of Māra,[56] does not bind his listeners with words, does not call himself a preceptor; his voice is like a resounding echo in the valley, and his preaching is all-pervading, faultless and trustworthy.

He who thinks he can preach and can expound (the Dharma) and says, 'I am a monk, you are my disciples' speaks the language of demons.

He who, without reason, says he sees the Tao prevailing and speaks of what *is* and what *is not* Buddha, what is bodhi, nirvāṇa, liberation and the like, indulges in pointless talk.

He who claims to know and to understand (the Dharma) and when seeing someone hold up a hand or raise a finger, hastens to declare 'this is Ch'an, this is Tao' delights in talking binding words which are precisely the rope that ties up a monk more tightly before he is firmly settled (for practice).

However, speechlessness is also faulty. It is far better to master the mind than to be mastered by it. The incomplete teaching (Hīnayāna) postulates the need of teachers of men and devas and of Nāyaka (pilots)[57] but the complete teaching (Mahāyāna) does not speak of teachers of men and devas and of reliance on Dharma as one's guide.

Before achieving a deep insight one should rely on the complete teaching to get close (to the Truth) for the incomplete teaching is suitable only for deaf worldlings.

Now if one does not cling to what *is* and what *is not*, also to this very idea of non-clinging, and to the awareness of this idea as well, one is a great man of good counsel (kalyāṇamitra). Hence, it is said, the Buddha alone is a great kalyāṇamitra,

56. This refers to the Vaiśeṣika-nikāya-daśapadārtha-śāstra of the Vaiśeṣika school of Indian philosophy, which teaches a dualism and an endless number of souls, and the doctrine of particularity or individual essence.

57. Nāyaka: a leader, guide, one who guides men to the truth; applied also to Buddhas and Bodhisattvas.

besides whom there is no second, for all others are heretics who speak the language of the demon.

You have only to preach the wiping out of all dualities and of all that *is* and *is not* and the keeping from desire, defilement and untying bondage, beyond which there is nothing to teach to others. If you say you can teach them and can bestow some Dharma upon them, this is heresy, also called the language of the demon.

Now you should distinguish between complete (Mahāyāna) and partial (Hīnayāna) truths, negating and non-negating terms,[58] living and dead meanings,[59] healing and injuring expressions,[60] accordant and discordant phrases,[61] and general and special words.[62]

Words such as: cultivation and attainment of Buddhahood, practice and realization, mind is Buddha, and identity of mind and Buddha are spoken by the Buddha to reveal the partial truth (Hīnayāna) and are non-negating, general and progressive terms of dead meaning used when teaching ignorant worldlings to sort out impurities (existing) according to worldly thinking.

Words such as: neither cultivation nor attainment of Buddhahood, neither practice nor realization, and neither mind nor Buddha, are also spoken by the Buddha to reveal the whole truth (Mahāyāna) and are negating, special, thrusting and discordant terms, beyond the three vehicles (of śrāvakas, pratyeka-buddhas and bodhisattvas), used to sort out purities when teaching saints from the stage of śrota-

58. Negating is denying what *is* or the seeming existence of things; and non-negating is acknowledging what *is* to look into its underlying nature.

59. Dead meaning of the seeming and living meaning of the real.

60. Healing refers to medicine that cures men of desire, hate and stupidity; and injuring refers to disease caused by desire, hate and stupidity.

61. Accordant to the worldly way of life to stay in the realm of birth and death; discordant from the worldly way of life to realize the absolute.

62. Collective karma or general characteristics of all phenomena; and individual karma or specific characteristics of different phenomena.

āpanna (entering the holy stream) to the tenth (or highest) degree of bodhisattva development into Buddhahood.

All words and speeches lead to defilement, kleśa (trouble) and incomplete revelation of the truth (Hīnayāna). Total revelation of reality (Mahāyāna) upholds the truth whereas partial revelation of reality (Hīnayāna) subverts the truth. Hence both partial and total revelations of reality are inhibited in the Buddha stage.

Just as earth can be appraised by looking at what grows in it, so can purity be appreciated by comparing it to turbidity.

But if mystic insight is reckoned on the basis of purity, the presence of this mystic insight is not purity and its absence is equally not purity for the mystic insight is neither holy nor unholy. For it is not like dirty water which can be indicated when it is actually seen. But if water is limpid nothing further should be said of it for the mere mention of it (as an object) can only make it dirty (by creating a duality in the mind).

If there be unquestioning query, there is also speechless reply.[63] If the Buddha does not regard himself as an enlightened one, his preaching is universal for in the absolute dharmadhātu[64] there is not a Buddha who does not liberate living beings. A Buddha not regarding himself as such is a true field of blessedness (for all living beings).

It is most important to distinguish the host from the guest, for if you cling to and are defiled by what *is* and what *is not*, you will be deluded and confused by these dual states in which your mind is the king of demons and its stirrings and wanderings are his subjects. If your mystic insight keeps from what *is* and what *is not*, from both the mundane and the supramundane, and also from both awareness and unawareness of so keeping away, your mind is Buddha and its shining

63. Cf The Vimalakīrti Nirdeśa Sūtra in which Vimalakīrti remained speechless in reply to Mañjuśrī's unquestioning query.
64. Dharmadhātu: the unifying underlying spiritual reality, the absolute from which all proceeds.

(wisdom) and (enlightened) functioning are his attendant Bodhisattvas.

For the mind is the stationary master and its manifestation and functioning are foreign dust (moving) like waves in relation to water which reflects all things without winning any merits therefrom.

If the mind is serene and radiates, and is free from the concept of its own abstruseness, it will pierce through the past and the present.[65] Hence it is said that spiritual shining without the notion of merits, wins the highest merit which is everlasting, with the qualification for (enlightened) guidance and leadership (nāyaka).

The consciousness of all living beings which has no access to the Buddha path has an adhesive nature for it clings to what *is* and what *is not*, and if by chance it hears the profound doctrine it fails to believe it for it is unfamiliar with the absolute.

Hence the Buddha passed 49 days under a bo-tree to meditate on prajñā (absolute wisdom) which is inexpressible and without compare.

For to say that all living beings possess the Buddha-nature is to defame the Three Precious Ones (Buddha, Dharma and Saṅgha), and to say that they do not possess it also defames the Three Precious Ones.[66]

To say there is Buddha-nature is defaming it by clinging to it (as real) and to say there is no Buddha-nature is defaming it by regarding it as fictitious.[67]

To say the Buddha-nature exists is defaming it by the groundless presumption of its advantage and to say the Buddha-nature is non-existent is defaming it by the baseless assumption of its disadvantage.[68]

To say the Buddha-nature is both existing and non-existent

65. i.e. unifying the past and the present to wipe out the element of time.
66. For the Buddha-nature can be neither owned nor unowned.
67. For the Buddha-nature is neither real nor unreal.
68. For the Buddha-nature is beyond gain and loss.

is self-contradiction, and to say it is neither existing nor non-existent is sheer sophistry.

So (immediately after his enlightenment) the Buddha first hesitated to reveal the truth to living beings, which would prevent their deliverance. But when he began to reveal it they clung to his words to make (wrong) interpretations which proved more harmful than beneficial. Hence he said, 'I would rather enter nirvāṇa forthwith than expound the Dharma.' He then pondered over examples set by past Buddhas who formulated the doctrine of three vehicles (of śrāvaka, pratyeka-buddha and Bodhisattva) and devised expedient terms which, though basically unfit to reveal (the absolute stages of) Buddha, bodhi, nirvāṇa and liberation, can be employed indirectly to suggest these indescribable and inexpressible states for personal experience and realization.

Knowing that they were too weak to lift up heavy weights and loads, he gave them pints and quarts to raise. Knowing that they were incapable of absorbing the whole truth (Mahāyāna) he revealed to them the partial truth so that (relative) good prevails for it is much better than evil. But when good (which is not everlasting) comes to an end, it is bound to be replaced by evil. (This is the case with all relativities and) if Buddhahood can be realized it is bound to be followed by (the state of) living beings. So if (relative) nirvāṇa can be attained it is bound to be followed by saṁsāra (the state of birth and death). If light appears it is bound to be followed by darkness. Therefore, all earthly causes and effects are bound to alternate with one another. To avoid their mutual dependence it is imperative to cut off both the extremes of all dualities by keeping from (the concepts of) Buddha and living being, near and distant relations, high and low (positions), equality and inequality, and coming and going. By not clinging to words and speeches, you will wipe out the two extremes of all dualities which will not hold you in bondage, in order to disengage yourselves from the mutual dependence of suffering and happiness and alternating light

75

and darkness so that reality is not (true) reality and that false-hood is not (real) falsehood because this (absolute state) is beyond all measure and estimate. It is like empty space which can be neither practised nor regulated. If you give rise to the least interpretation of it you will be immediately conditioned by measure and estimate. This is like ill luck caused by the evil influence of opposition by the five elements[69] or like the glue that sticks the five senses, and you will be caught and led away by the king of demons.

The teaching on the three progressive stages of initial, intermediate and final excellence, formulates the development of the excellent mind in the first stage, the wiping out of it in the second stage so that the absolute one emerges in the third stage in which (the student will understand the Buddha's profound words in the Diamond Sūtra, such as) 'the Bodhisattva is not real but is so-called expediently (for teaching purposes)' and 'the Dharma is neither Dharma nor not Dharma.'[70]

If you teach only one of these three stages to living beings, you will cause them to fall into the hells, but after you have taught them all three, if they fall into hells by themselves, this has nothing to do with the Lord's teaching (which is not wrong).

Your actual introspection into your (inner) self-Buddha is the first excellent stage; your non-holding on to this intro-spection is the intermediate excellent stage; and your freedom from this idea of non-holding on to it is the ultimate excellent stage.

So the preceding (or fundamental inner) Buddha is Dipaṁkara Buddha[71] and the following (or developing) Buddha (e.g. Śākyamuni Buddha) is neither wordly nor

69. The five elements of metal, wood, water, fire and earth used in divination in China.

70. Cf *Ch'an and Zen Teaching, First Series*, part III, The Diamond Cutter of Doubts. (Rider, London; Shambala, Berkeley).

71. Lit. 'The Illuminating Lamp', the twenty fourth predecessor of

saintly, but do not make the mistake of saying that this Buddha is neither a worldling nor a saint.[72]

The First Patriarch of this land[73] said, 'He who is neither mighty nor saintly is the Buddha- (or Enlightened) Saint.' But when you speak of this Buddha-saint, he does not belong to any of the nine classes of spiritual beings such as dragons, animals, etc., for you know that in past and present aeons these beings have never been and will never be Buddhas. You know also that the asuras have bodies twice the size of mount Sumeru and that when they fought Śakra and realized that they could not win, they led millions of their warriors into hiding in the holes of lotus roots; they could thus make transformations and also had the power of speech, but they were not Buddhas.

The technical terms devised for the teaching have various meanings and are divided into different categories to be used either lavishly or scantily and for the purpose of lifting or lowering their significances. For instance, that which was called desire and hatred before awakening becomes the Buddha-wisdom after enlightenment. Hence the saying, 'It is the same man as before, the only difference lies in his common acts of daily life.'

*

One day someone asked the master, 'Do the acts of mowing grass, felling trees and reclaiming barren lands bring retribution?'[74]

The master replied, 'You cannot say for sure if these acts

Śākyamuni who foretold the latter's attainment of Buddhahood. Cf *Ch'an and Zen Teaching, First Series*, pages 172 and 190. (Rider, London; Shambala, Berkeley)

72. Because this implies the duality of subjective Buddha and objective saint and worldling.

73. Bodhidharma was the First Ch'an Patriarch in China.

74. Acts which agree with bodhi.

will bring retribution or not for this depends on each individual case. If one is contaminated by what *is* and what *is not* and still discriminates between the acceptance and rejection of things, that is if one cannot pass through the three stages of excellent mind (as previously described) one cannot escape from retribution.

But he who leaps over and beyond these three stages with a mind empty like space and free from this very idea of empty space, he is sure to be free from retribution.'

The master continued, 'There is no such thing as freedom from retribution after one has committed an offense. Equally there is no such thing as retribution when one does not commit any offences.

According to the vinaya[75] there is no retribution if in self-defence one kills a murderer who threatens one's life. How much more so is our Ch'an sect which formulates a mind void (immaterial) and containing nothing, which is above and beyond the notion of voidness; where then can retribution be found in it?

It is also said that the Ch'an path is beyond practice; one has only to keep from pollution.

It is also said that you have only to dissolve both outer and inner minds[76] until both vanish and then you will achieve liberation.

It is also said that when confronted with externals (sense data) you should keep from all that *is* and *is not* with no desire of and attachment to anything.

It is also said that (ch'an) practice is like washing dirty clothes; the clothes are what you originally possess and the dirt comes from without. When you hear about what *is* and what *is not*, about sound and form, these are like the dirt which should not be retained.

75. Vinaya: one of the three divisions of Mahāyāna canon which teaches the rules of morality and discipline, the other two being sūtra (sermons) and śāstra (treatises)

76. External sense data and internal sense organs.

The thirty-two unsurpassed physical marks and eighty accompanying excellent characteristics (of the Buddha) sitting under the bo-tree, are forms and the twelve divisions of (Mahāyāna) sermons are sounds; all you have to do is to cut off the stream of all that *is* and of all that *is not*, of form and sound, thus emptying your mind so that it is like the void. You must learn how to do so with the same eagerness of a man hastening to save his burning head,[77] and only then will you succeed.

'At death one may not even find and follow familiar old tracks; therefore, if one waits until then to practise a new and unfamiliar Dharma, one cannot expect satisfactory results. (But as a result of one's habitual practice) one will be confronted with only good states and one's predilection for any one of them will determine one's future lot. Since one has refrained from evil, no evil states will manifest and even if they appear they will always change into good ones.

If one fears that at the time of death one may take fright at one's helplessness and loss of freedom, one should learn to be free right now while alive. If one is now free from desire of, and contamination by, every state encountered, with no awareness of that freedom from such desire and contamination, one will be a real free man. The present conduct is cause and what manifests at the time of death is effect. So

77. This analogy has never before been translated into English: probably it seems strange to some modern pundits in the East as well as in the West.

We have been unfairly criticized for presenting it in our writings, but prefer to be criticized than to drop this ancient Indian analogy between a Buddhist eager to save himself from the misery of life and a man hastening to save his burning head. As a faithful translator, we are used to and can endure groundless criticism and attack, provided the cause of the Dharma is served.

Moreover, many Indians wear turbans which can catch fire and there is nothing strange to them when they read this analogy in Mahāyāna sūtras. In modern warfare, napalm bombs are frequently dropped on the enemy and those who have seen this will not criticize a soldier striving to save his burning head.

when the fruit of the karma ripens and manifests, what can your fear accomplish?

Your fear is about the past and present. If the past existed because (of its dependence on) the present, the present also exists because (of its dependence on) the past. If there were Buddhas in the past, there are also Buddhas in the present. If one wins liberation in the present, one will win it in the future (and for ever). Therefore, every one of your thoughts should be disengaged from what *is* and what *is not*. In the past as well as at present, a Buddha was and is just a man and a man can become a Buddha. This is like the imperturbable samādhi and there is no need to use a samādhi to enter the state of samādhi. (Likewise) dhyāna should not be used to seek dhyāna, and a Buddha should not be employed to search for another Buddha.

Hence it is said that if Dharma does not seek Dharma, if Dharma does not win Dharma, if Dharma does not function as Dharma and if Dharma does not perceive Dharma, real Dharma will automatically be realized, but once realized it cannot be realized for a second time.

Therefore, a Bodhisattva should hold the correct view of an entirely solitary Dharma, forsaking even this very idea of its solitariness, and the nature of his wisdom will become absolute by itself and independent from all causes. This is called the formation of his (enlightened) substance and also the gathering of this substance which cannot be discerned by his intellect and known by his consciousness, being above and beyond all thinking and estimating until this serene substance is no more and all mental activities cease for ever, like rivers and streams that flow into the vast ocean to merge in its deep water without further rippling its surface.

This is like ripples on the sea in windless weather. Your sudden awareness of them is a coarse aspect among the fine ones, and your (subsequent) indifference to this awareness is the most subtle aspect among the subtle ones, which is the Buddha stage. This initial awareness is called the highest samādhi, also called the sovereign samādhi and basic wisdom (jñeya), the begetter of all the states of samādhi that ordain all Bodhisattvas so that all form, sound, smell, taste, touch, dharma, and lands will contribute to their achievement of supreme enlightenment which is unobstructed both within and without.

So every form, every speck of dust, and every Buddha and all forms, all specks of dust, all Buddhas and all sense data fill all the lands (in the ten directions); this is the coarse aspect among the fine ones, and is an excellent state of seeing, hearing, feeling and knowing of the highest order; a stage in the realm of birth and death to wipe out what *is* and what *is not*; a preaching of the highest degree, the lofty nirvāṇa, the unsurpassed Tao, the unequalled mantra,[78] the most exalted and most profound of all sermons which is not accessible to men and enjoys the protection (blessing) of all Buddhas.

This is like a transparent wave which reveals the limpidity and turbidity of all waves. The depth and extensiveness of (the Dharma's) functioning enjoys the protection of all Buddhas, and if you can preserve it while walking, standing, sitting and reclining, I shall always appear in my bright, radiant, pure and clean bodily form (to receive you).'

The master continued, 'Like you who can thus realize this universal (mind) and its universal expression, I am also (in the absolute state). (Therefore), every sound, smell, taste, touch and thought is all-embracing everywhere in the world and in all the extensive lotus realm of every Buddha.[79]

However, if you cling to this initial awareness as your correct interpretation, this is the worst knot, also called a fall into the most dangerous entanglement which is the root of all troubles (kleśa). This self-created perverse view ties one

78. Quote from the Heart Sūtra. Cf *Ch'an and Zen Teaching, First Series*, page 219 (Rider, London; Shambala, Berkeley).

79. The lotus realm or lotus treasury of every Buddha for his sam-bhogakaya, e.g. the Western Paradise of Bliss is the lotus world of Amitābha Buddha.

up even without a rope. This barrier of the known involves twenty-five forms of existence[80] holding them all in bondage and spreads troubles (kleśa) everywhere.

This initial awareness is called jñeya (the root of knowledge) by Hīnayāna men, and is also a very subtle kleśa which should be uprooted at once. After this uprooting of subtle kleśa, spirit returns to its empty abode which is also called intoxication by the liquor of (false) samādhi. It is also called bondage by the demon of (wrong) liberation.

Since the formation and destruction of a world are caused by this power of maladjusted stillness which leads the neophyte to another world of existence without his awareness of it, this is the deep pit of (false) liberation which is frightful and from which all Bodhisattvas carefully keep away.

This is also called a fall that makes him a god-ruler (cakravartī) who urges the inhabitants of the four heavens to perform every day ten good actions[81] the merits of which are incalculable.

For introspection is a regal cause which, if linked to what *is* and what *is not* makes him a cakravartī. However, if he can prevent the concept of *is* and *is not* from entering his body, and keep it above and beyond the four expressions of differentiation,[82] this is called voidness (śūnyatā) which is the medicine of immortality that makes the cakravartī immortal. Although it is called the medicine of immortality, if the cakravartī takes it both he and the medicine are neither two different things (diversity) nor a single one (unity).

But if a neophyte discriminates between unity and diversity, he also will be a cakravartī.

Now if someone, besides giving the four necessaries of

80. The 25 forms of existence: 14 in the worlds of desire, 7 in the worlds of form, and 4 in the formless worlds.

81. The ten good virtues are the non-committal of the ten evils: killing, stealing, carnality, lying, double-tongue, coarse language, affected speech, covetousness, anger and perverted views.

82. Is, is not, both, either, or phenomenal, noumenal, both, neither.

life[83] bestows also blessedness and wisdom to living beings of the four types of birth[84] in the six worlds of existence[85] as many as the incalculable number of 4 million lacs of asankyas[86] and if after so satisfying their needs for 80[87] years he thinks of their decay and old age, and says to himself, "I should now teach them the Buddha Dharma so that they can realize the successive stages from srota-āpanna to arhatship". This patron who first only provides them with all means to worldly happiness, already reaps countless merits; how much more so when he helps them to attain to the stages of srota-āpanna up to arhatship, but his limitless merits are still much less than those earned by the fiftieth man who rejoices at hearing about the Buddha vehicle.[88]

The Sūtra on Requiting Favours says that Mahāmāyā[89] had 500 sons all realizing pratyeka-buddahood and after their nirvāṇa when stūpas were erected to worship them, she sighed and said, "It would have been far better to have had one single son who realized supreme bodhi and would have thus saved me all the troubles."

This is like a disciple who from among hundreds, thousands and tens of thousands of aspirants, wins that which (exceeds in value) all the three great chiliocosms. Hence I always urge you all to awaken to the profundity of your self-nature, and

83. The four necessaries of life: dwelling, clothing, victuals and medicine.
84. The four types of birth: from wombs, eggs, humidity and by transformation.
85. Worlds of devas, asuras, men, animals, hungry ghosts and hells.
86. Innumerable aeons. The digit 4 stands for the four elements that make the physical body.
87. The digit 8 stands for the eight consciousnesses.
88. Quote from the Lotus Sūtra which tells of someone who, after the nirvāṇa of the Buddha, rejoices at hearing this sūtra and spreads it to others until the fiftieth man who also rejoices at hearing it. The merits won by this last man are already incalculable. How much more so are those reaped by the first man who transmits this sūtra to forty-nine other men.
89. The Buddha's mother, also called Māyā.

if you perceive it as very abstruse, you will win blessedness and wisdom, like a master commanding all his servants. This is also likened to a non-stop cart.

But if you cling to your interpretation (without attempting to advance further) this is like a precious pearl (hidden) in the topknot, like a precious stone with a fixed price and like taking excrement into the body.[90] If you do not cling to your understanding, this is like the donation of a luminous pearl to adorn the prince's topknot, like a priceless precious stone, and like taking excrement out of the body. Buddha is a man free from all bondage but worldlings use bondage to bind (their minds) within. If you want to realize Buddhahood in this manner, you are worldlings on the shore of birth and death, where the (abstruse) truth is interrupted.

If you want to realize Buddahood on this shore (of unenlightenment) this is impossible for men and monkeys. Men stand for the Bodhisattvas of the ten stages and monkeys for worldlings.

You are not forbidden to read sūtras and study the Dharma in order to understand and interpret the teaching of the three vehicles (of śrāvakas, pratyeka-buddhas and Bodhisattvas) with a view to embellishing yourselves with necklaces of precious stones[91] and to acquire the thirty-two excellent physical marks,[92] but you will fail in your quest for enlightenment in a household cave.[93]

The teaching says, "You are not even allowed to frequent Hinayāna men". Still less can you meet monks who have broken the prohibitions and arhats in name and not in reality. For these bad monks and false arhats commit evils comparable to the hunting and fishing mentioned in the Mahāparinirvāṇa

90. Quote from the Lotus Sūtra which tells of worldlings who take in excrements, i.e. who allow sense data to enter and delude their minds.

91. Precious stones stand for moral excellences.

92. Cf *Ch'an and Zen Teaching, First Series*, page 178 note 2. (Rider, London; Shambala, Berkeley).

93. i.e. with a conditioned mind.

ωûtra which lists sixteen categories of bad karmas resulting from injuring and killing living beings for food or pecuniary gains.[94]

Mahāyāna and Vaipulya (expanded sūtras) are the elixir of immortality and are also like poison. If they can be absorbed and digested they are the elixir of life but if they are not digested they are poison.

When you read the sūtras and study their teachings, if you do not discern their dead (literal) from their living meanings, you will certainly fail to understand their deep import. It is, therefore, far better not to read the sūtras.'

The master added, 'You should study the teaching and also call on men of good counsel (kalyāṇamitra). It is most important to develop your mind's eye in order to be clear about both the dead and living meanings (of words used in the teaching). If you do not see clearly, you will fail to understand it thoroughly and will only increase your own obstructions.

Hence those who teach the profound meaning (of the teaching) do not forbid the reading of sūtras. If they uphold the essence (i.e. the underlying nature) instead of the form, and the deep meaning instead of the style, such a preaching is a correct one, for preaching (the literal meaning of) words and letters vilifies (the Dharma) and is called heterodoxy.

If a Bodhisattva says, "You should preach according to the Dharma" his is also correct preaching, for he urges living beings to control their minds instead of phenomena, to regulate their conduct instead of sense data, to preach the (absolute) self instead of (empty) words, and the living instead of dead or literal meaning, and to say that dhyāna does not prevail in

94. According to the Mahāparinirvāṇa Sūtra the 16 categories of evil karmas result from: 1 to 8, feeding lambs, pigs, calves and chickens until they grow fat and then sell them for pecuniary gain, and buying and killing them for food for sale, also for pecuniary gain; 9, catching fish; 10, hunting; 11, plundering; 12, the occupation of an executioner; 13, netting birds for sale; 14, double tongue; 15, the occupation of a jailer; and 16, cursing nāgas.

the world of desire; all this is the preaching by one who has developed the mind's eye.

If dhyāna does not prevail in the realm of desire, by which means does one reach the realm of form? First from the causal ground (i.e. the realm of desire) one should practise two kinds of stillness in order to reach the first dhyāna heaven: the thoughtful stillness and the thoughtless stillness. The thoughtful stillness ensures rebirth in the four heavenly regions of the realm of form, and the thoughtless stillness ensures rebirth in the four formless heavens.[95] It is, therefore, clear that dhyāna does not prevail in the realm of desire for it exists only in the realms of form (and beyond form).'

Question. 'If so why is it said that dhyāna exists in this world?'

Answer. 'The absence of both disturbance and dhyāna is the Tathāgata-dhyāna which keeps from the idea of developing dhyāna.

Question. 'What is the meaning of the saying, "Where there is passion there is no Buddha-nature, and where there is no passion there is Buddha-nature?"'

Answer. 'The conception of men up to the Buddha stage is clinging to holy passion and that of men down to the hells is clinging to worldly passion.'

Now clinging to both the worldly and saintly states is the presence of passion with the absence of Buddha-nature. If your mind neither accepts nor rejects both the worldly and saintly states, and all that *is* and *is not*, and is free from this very idea of acceptance and rejection, as well as from the awareness of such freedom, this is the absence of passion with the presence of Buddha-nature.

The absence of passion means freedom from bondage caused by passion, but does not mean that a piece of wood, a stone, empty space, a yellow flower or a green bamboo which are passionless, possess the Buddha-nature. If you insist that

95. Cf *The Śūrṅgama Sutra* pages 192–196 (Rider, London).

86

they all possess the Buddha-nature, why have you not found in the sūtras the Buddha's prediction of their future realization of Buddhahood?

Now if your introspection cannot be changed by passion, this is likened to the green bamboo (which does not change colour) and if your introspection responds (to the Dharma) and knows the ripening time (of your bodhi) this is like the yellow flower (that foretells the season).'

The master added: 'Treading the Buddha-path is the absence of passion with the presence of Buddha-nature but if the Buddha-path is not yet trodden, this is the presence of passion with the absence of Buddha-nature.'

Miscellaneous Sayings of Pai Chang

A monk asked the master, 'The Buddha Mahābhijñā-jñānābhibhu spent ten kalpas (aeons) in sitting on a bodhi-maṇḍala (i.e. sitting in meditation) during which the Buddha Dharma did not manifest, and so failed to realize Buddhahood.[96] Why was it so?'

The master replied, 'Kalpa stands for *stagnation* and also for *dwelling*. If one's (mind) dwells in any one of the ten good virtues[97] it will stagnate in all the ten. The Indian word "Buddha" means "the enlightened one." If one's introspection clings to good virtues, one is a man of good root who does not possess the Buddha-nature. Hence "the Buddha Dharma did not manifest and so he failed to realize Buddhahood".[98]

'He who when confronting evil dwells in it, develops the

96. Quote from the Lotus Sūtra, chapter 7. This Buddha later achieved supreme enlightenment after the tenth kalpa. Cf *Ch'an and Zen Teaching, Second Series*, The Seal of the Precious Mirror Samādhi, page 153 and note 1. (Rider, London; Shambala, Berkeley).

97. The non-committal of ten evils. See page 82 note 81.

98. Because of expectation of enlightenment which hinders its realization.

awareness of a living being. He who when confronting good dwells in it, develops the śrāvaka awareness. He who considers his non-dwelling in the duality of good and evil to be correct, develops the pratyeka-buddha awareness. He who not only keeps from dwelling in the duality of good and evil but also foresakes the concept of this non-dwelling, develops the Bodhisattva awareness. He who not only keeps from (all) dwelling and also from this idea of non-dwelling, develops the Buddha awareness.

He who has realized Buddhahood and does not dwell in this (objective) enlightened state, is a real field of blessedness (for all living beings). Of the thousands, and tens of thousands of men, if someone realizes this absolute state, he is a priceless gem, a real leader of all, who turns the great Wheel of the Law by proclaiming Buddha where there is no (objective) Buddha, Dharma where there is no (objective) Dharma and Saṅgha where there is no (objective) Saṅgha'.

*

Someone asked the master, '(It is said that) the Patriarch's sect transmitted esoteric words orally from one master to another; what does this mean?'

The master replied, 'There are no esoteric words and the Tathāgata does not possess an esoteric store. Now if your introspection shows that your words and speeches are free from form and appearance, they are esoteric expressions. From the stage of śrota-āpanna up to the ten stages of Bodhisattva (development into Buddhahood) all words and speeches pertain to the defiling dust, to the shore of kleśa and to the partial revelation of the truth (Hīnayāna) and are inhibited and refuted in the complete revelation of reality (Mahāyāna). So what esoteric words do you want to know?'

The questioner. '(It is said that) the void in the supreme bodhi is likened to a bubble forming in the sea. What does this mean?'

The master. 'The void is likened to the bubble and the sea

88

to the self-nature. The enlightened spiritual self-nature is vast and contains the void; hence the void in the supreme bodhi is likened to a bubble forming in the sea.'

The questioner. 'What is the meaning of the saying, "Fell the forest but not the tree?"'

The master. 'The forest stands for the mind and the tree for the body. Speaking of the forest causes an alarm, hence "fell the forest but not the tree" (to lay stress on disciplining the mind which is the prime mover of the body).'

The questioner. 'Words are like targets which invite hitting arrows. If words are targets, they are not without trouble. In view of the trouble which is created in all cases, how does one discern what is right from what is wrong?'

The master. 'When arrows are shot forward they follow one after another unless one of them leaves the course causing itself or something to be hit.

Therefore, trying to find the form of an echo in a ravine is futile in spite of countless aeons passed for the purpose, for it is just a repetition of a voice coming from your own mouth. What is right and wrong originates from your (discriminating) question the core of which is an (illusory) arrow. If this arrow is known to be only an illusion, that which knows this illusion, will no longer be illusory.

The Third Patriarch said:

> If mind's profoundness you ignore
> You can never practise stillness.[99]

He also said:

> If you take objects to see
> It is like keeping potsherds
> For of what use are they?
> If you say that you see nothing
> You differ not from wood and stone.

99. Cf *Practical Buddhism*, page 35. (Rider, London; The Theosophical Publishing House, Wheaton, USA).

Therefore, seeing and not seeing are both wrong; this illustrates the falsehood in all cases'.

The questioner. 'If fundamentally there be no kleśa, why are there the thirty-two (unsurpassed) physical marks (of a Buddha).'

The master. 'This pertains to the Buddha state. For fundamentally there are kleśa and the thirty-two physical marks appear now to reveal worldly passion (but they do not exist in the absolute suchness).'

The questioner. 'What is the meaning of the saying that the Bodhisattva of Boundless Body does not see the top of the Tathāgata's head?'

The master. 'It is because of discrimination between bounded and boundless vision that the top of the Tathāgata's head is not seen. Now if you keep from (all dualities such as) what *is* and what *is not* and also from this very idea of so keeping from them, the top of the Tathāgata's head will appear to you.'

The questioner. 'Nowadays all monks say that they agree with the Buddha's teaching in their study (and practice) of sūtras, śāstras, dhyāna, vinaya, knowledge and interpretation; are they qualified to receive the four necessaries of life (offered by their patrons)?'[100]

The master. 'He who, in his daily perception of every sound, form, smell, taste and everything that *is* and *is not*, keeps from all clinging thereto and contamination therefrom, also from the very idea of non-clinging as well as from the awareness of such an idea, is qualified to spend each day ten thousand ounces of pure gold on a feast which can be easily digested.'[101]

'When encountering what *is* and what *is not* you have only

100. See page 83 note 83 for explanation.

101. The Chinese term 'digest' means that the man is qualified to enjoy an expensive feast. On the other hand 'he does digest it' if he is not entitled to it.

to disengage your six sense organs from both, but if you still entertain the least desire and liking (for them) - even your begging for a grain of rice or a shred of thread, will involve you in an indebtedness which must be repaid or in default, a retributory rebirth as a haired or horned pack or plough animal to requite it before you can aspire to be a non-relying Buddha. For Buddha is a non-clinging man, is a non-seeking man and is a free man.[102] Because of your restlessness in your search for Buddha you turn your back on him.

Hence the saying, "You have been close to the Buddha for a very long time but still ignore the Buddha-nature." The Buddha, only after passing through the six realms of existence in saṁsāra for a very long time, perceived the state of Buddha-hood and then said, "It is indeed very difficult to meet the Buddha."

Mañjuśri who was a tutor of seven Buddhas, also said, "I am the highest chief Bodhisattva in the realm of sahā, but for merely thinking about the perception of Buddha and the hearing of Dharma, under the influence of the Buddha-power, I was downgraded to stay on the second iron-mountain."[103] This does not mean that he did not understand the Dharma, for he made these mistakes on purpose to teach future students to avoid wrong seeing and wrong hearing. But if you keep from what *is* and what *is not* and from the idea of these dualities so that you can pass beyond the threefold eradication (of coarse, fine and finest clingings)[104], this state is called

102. This involves three separate meditations, first on non-clinging, then on non-seeking and finally on freeing oneself from all reliance, and each phase may take some time to master. The English seems to be clumsy but the meaning is not.

103. Cakravāla or cakravāḍa, the iron enclosing mountains that encircle the earth, forming the periphery of a world. Mount Sumeru is the centre and between it and the iron mountains, are the seven metal-mountains and the eight seas.

104. See page 76.

cintāmaṇi[105] and also is walking on flowers."[106] However, if you cling to the view of Buddha and Dharma and of what *is* and what *is not*, this is (the duality of subjective) seeing and (objective) things seen through an optical illusion. Because of this duality of the seeing and the seen, this is also called visionary hindrance or screened sight or retributory vision.

Now if every thought of yours about seeing, hearing, feeling and knowing and about all defiling dust, is driven away so that every speck of dust and every form turn into Buddha and that each rising thought is solely about Buddha; in the three periods of time and through the five aggregates these thoughts will follow one another to become countless Buddhas who will crowd in the empty space; this is the Buddha power to reproduce himself (ad infinitum and everywhere), also called a gemmed stūpa.

Hence the usual lamentation of those whose lives depend on food (and drink) and who will starve to death if they have nothing to eat, will die from thirst if they are deprived of drink and will perish from cold (in winter) for lack of heating; who cannot be born one day earlier and cannot die one day later, and who are at the mercy of the four elements (of earth, water, fire and air). It is therefore, far better to be one who has realized (bodhi) and who can enter a blaze without being scorched by fire, who can plunge into water without being drowned; who could be scorched if he wanted to be scorched, who could be drowned if he wanted to be drowned, who could live if he wanted to live and could die if he wanted to die; who is free to stay or leave at will; this is a man entitled to enjoy sovereign independence.

If the mind is unstirred there is no need to seek Buddha, Bodhi and Nirvāṇa for the search for Buddha is a desire which becomes a (spiritual) illness. Hence the saying that "the

105. A gem capable of responding to every wish.
106. All Buddhas and Bodhisattvas are said to walk in space, with precious lotus flowers under their feet.

Buddha-illness is very difficult to cure." "If you defame the (objective) Buddha, break the (objective) Law (Dharma) . . . then you can take away the food and eat it."[107] Eating (here) refers to feeding one's spiritual enlightened nature with the food of passionless liberation, and these few words cure the illness of all the ten stages of Bodhisattva (development) from the first to the tenth. Those whose minds search for all things are law-breaking bhikṣus and arhats in name but not in reality; they are all jackals, and obviously are not qualified to take offerings from their patrons.

Now he who hears a voice as if it were an echo and smells a fragrance as if it were the odourless wind, who keeps from all that *is* and that *is not*, also from the very idea of so keeping away, and likewise from the knowledge of this (mental) attitude, is a man who is free from all spiritual defilement; in his quest for supreme enlightenment and nirvāṇa, even if he is called a (true) leaver of home, his (intentional quest for bodhi) is still an heretical vow. How much more so are worldly disputation, discrimination between success and failure, self-praise of ability and understanding for the purpose of winning a disciple's respect or a student's attachment; of securing a patron who will provide one with shelter, clothes and food, and of acquiring fame and money by boasting of one's achievements free from all obstructions which show only self-deception.

Now if one disowns the five aggregates and is free from resentment, hatred and trouble (kleśa) even when one's body is mutilated[108] or if one is free from a single thought of the self and others, when seeing one's own disciple being badly beaten from head to foot by (evil) men, and so holds on to (the objective) thoughtlessness which one regards as correct

107. Quote from *The Vimalakīrti Nirdeśa Sūtra* page 27. (Shambala, Berkeley; Routledge, London).

108. Quote from the Diamond Sūtra. Cf *Ch'an and Zen Teaching, First Series*, part III, The Diamond Cutter of Doubts, page 182 last para. (Rider, London; Shambala, Berkeley).

(in both cases); this is called a defiling mental object which the Bodhisattvas of the ten stages (of development into Buddhahood) have great difficulty in driving away and which is the cause of a fall into the flowing river of birth and death.

Hence I always urge my listeners to keep from trouble (kleśa) caused by defiling mental objects with the same fear of (rebirth in) the three realms of misery[109] before they can aspire to win liberation. He who refrains from prizing something that even surpasses nirvāṇa, follows in the Buddha's footsteps and need not walk in space with lotus flowers under his feet to appear in countless transformation bodies. Now if you still have an atom of fondness for what *is* and what *is not*, even if you walk on lotus flowers in space, your act does not differ from a demon's.

He who clings to the interpretation of that which is basically pure, clean and free as a real Buddha and the true Ch'an path, is a heretic who denies the law of causality and holds that things happen spontaneously.

He who clings to causal practice and effectual realization is a heretic who holds the wrong view that bodhi originates from cause and effect.

He who clings to existence is a heretic holding the wrong view of permanence; and he who clings to non-existence is a heretic holding the wrong view of annihilation.

He who clings to the wrong concept of what either *is* or *is not* is a heretic holding the two extreme views of annihilation and immortality.

He who clings to the wrong concept of what neither *is* nor *is not* is a heretic holding the wrong view that karma and nirvāṇa are not real; he is also called a stupid heretic.

Now if one is free from the views of Buddha and nirvāṇa, and of all that *is* and *is not*, and also from the absence of such views, this is called right viewing. If one is free from all

109. The three unhappy worlds of animals, hungry ghosts and hells.

hearing and also from the absence of hearing, this is called
right hearing. All this is called triumphing over all heresies,
which prevents the demons of the human world from coming
(to disturb one); it is also called the great supernatural
mantra[110] which prevents the demons of the Hīnayāna stage
from coming; the great bright mantra[110] which prevents the
demons of the Bodhisattva stage from coming; the great
unsurpassed mantra[110] which prevents the demons of the
Buddha stage from coming; and the great unequalled
mantra[110] which first transforms the crooked asuras of this
world, then those of the Hīnayāna stage and finally the
crooked asuras of the Bodhisattva stage into what is called
the three transformations into pure lands.[111]

For all dualities such as what *is* and *is not*, the saintly and
the worldly, etc., are like gold ore whereas the absolute suchness is like pure gold. When the ore and its gold contents are
separated, pure gold is manifest to us. Then if someone wants
gold coins, the pure gold can be used to make them for him.

It is also like unmixed flour; if some poor man begs for
cakes, this flour can be used to make them for him.

It is also like an intelligent minister who knows his prince's
desires. When the prince is about to go out and consults his

110. Quote from the Heart Sūtra which says, 'So we know that Prajñā-
pāramitā is the great supernatural mantra, the great bright, unsurpassed
and unequalled mantra which can truly and without fail wipe out all
sufferings.' Cf *Ch'an and Zen Teaching, First Series*, page 219 (Rider,
London; Shambala, Berkeley).

111. The three transformations made by the Buddha on the Vulture
peak – first, his revelation of this world, then its transformation into two
million lacs of nayutas of countries and then the transformation of these
countless countries into pure-lands. Cf The Lotus Sūtra.

We prefer to translate according to the text of the Lotus Sūtra as above
instead of using the usual English words 'countless countries' for the
digit '2' (in two million lacs) stands for dualities which cause the unenlightenment of men, asuras, Hīnayāna men, and newly-initiated Bodhisattvas. This note is added to forestall criticism to which the author has
been subjected since the publication of his books.

cintāmaṇi[112] the minister brings him the horse; and when the prince takes his meal and consults his cintāmaṇi the minister brings him (table) salt.

The above examples illustrate a student of the profound doctrine who can enter all responsive states without fail; he is called a lion which has broken all the shackles of its six senses.

Ch'an master Pao Chih[113] said, 'Every man is subject to changes according to what he does but the Bodhisattva of the tenth stage suffers neither from hunger nor gluttony and can be neither drowned when entering water nor scorched when entering a fire. Since he cannot be scorched, to scorch him is running counter to fate (which protects him from suffering). But a Buddha differs from the former; if he wants to be scorched he can be scorched, and if he wants to be drowned he can be drowned. For he masters the four elements and is free from all geomantic influences,[114] and to him all forms are Buddha-forms and all sounds are Buddha-sounds.'[115]

He who has uprooted the impure and crooked mind thereby passing through and beyond the three stages of purification[116] can speak the (above) words.

A disciple of the Bodhisattva stage of purity and cleanness is clear about his words and speeches, refrains from clinging to (the duality of) *is* and *is not*, and is free in his application of shining wisdom and enlightening function which is not restrained by the concept of purity and impurity.

112. A talisman, a pearl granting all one's wishes.

113. Pao Chih: a Ch'an master at the time of emperor Liang Wu Ti (502–547 A.D.)

114. Lit. geomantic influences of wind and water.

115. Form and sound emanate from underlying nature and he who achieves a deep insight into form and sound is thereby enlightened.

116. The three stages of purification: first development of the pure mind, then non-dwelling in it and finally unmindfulness of even this non-dwelling. See also page 76.

He who is ill but refuses medicine is a stupid man. He who is not ill but takes medicine is a śrāvaka. He who clings to any aspect of the Dharma is a śrāvaka with a settled mind. He who is only keen to widen his knowledge (of the Dharma without putting it into practice) is an arrogant śrāvaka.[117] He who knows only technical terms is called a śrāvaka who still needs teaching and training. He who sinks into the void and likes stillness thereby knowing (only) himself is a śrāvaka who needs no further studies.

Desire, anger and stupidity are poison and the twelve divisions of the Mahāyāna canon are medicine. If the poison is not eliminated, one cannot stop taking the medicine. If medicine is taken when one is not ill, it will change into (or cause) an illness, but when this illness comes to an end, the medicine taken will not dissolve (i.e. will not be digested). That which is neither created nor destroyed is impermanence.[118]

The Mahāparinirvāṇā Sūtra says, 'There are three evil desires: the first is to be surrounded by the four vargas;[119] the second is to have all men as one's disciples; and the third is to have all men recognize one as a saint and an arhat.'

The Mahākāśyapa Sūtra says, 'The first desire is to see the coming Buddha; the second desire is to seek a cakravartī;[120] the third desire is to be a kṣatriya;[121] and the fourth desire is to be a Brahmin;[122] these as well as those for the hatred for birth and death and the quest for Nirvāṇa, are all evil desires which should be wiped out first.

117. Quote from the Lotus Sūtra which mentions 6,000 disciples who refused to listen to the Buddha's expounding of this sūtra because they thought they had acquired a complete knowledge of the Dharma.

118. Cf *Ch'an and Zen Teaching, Third Series*, part I, The Sūtra of the Sixth Patriarch, page 83. (Rider, London; Shambala, Berkeley)

119. The four vargas: monks, nuns, male and female devotees.

120. Cakravartī: a ruling god over a universe, a ruler the wheels of whose chariot roll everywhere without hindrance.

121. A warrior or ruling caste.

122. The highest caste in India.

Now all cravings are evil desires which pertain to the six heavens of desires[123] under the control of Pāpiyān.[124]

*

A questioner. 'What is the meaning of (the sentence) For twenty years, the youth was ordered to sweep clean the excrement (in the body)'?[125]

The master. 'Just put an end to all that *is* and *is not* as well as to all desires and cravings so that one can pass through and beyond the three stages of purification[126], this is sweeping clean the excrement (in the body)'.

Now if you seek Buddhahood, bodhi and all that *is* and *is not*, this is called taking excrement into the body but not out of it. If you hold the view of Buddha and interpret the (word) Buddha as an object to be perceived and sought, this is the excrement of sophistry, also called coarse language, or dead words.

Ordinary phrases (used in the sūtras) such as 'the ocean does not keep corpses' etc.,[127] do not pertain to sophistry, (but) words that swing between (contraries such as) purity and turbidity are sophisms.

The teaching classifies all things into twenty-one categories[128] for sifting and picking out the entangling defilements of all living beings.

123. Cf *The Śūraṅgama Sūtra*, page 190 (Rider, London).

124. Pāpiyān: the Evil One.

125. Quote from the Lotus Sūtra which means ridding oneself of discriminations and defilements to purify the mind.

126. See page 96 note 116.

127. One of the eight marvellous characteristics of the ocean, namely: its gradual increasing depth, its unfathomableness, its universal saltness, its regular tides, its store of precious things, its enormous creatures, its objection to corpses, its unvarying level despite all that pours into it. The Avataṁsaka Sūtra adds two more to the above eight, i.e. all other waters lose their names in it and its vastness of expanse.

128. All things are compounds possessing no self-essence, i.e. are

Pure living, the rules of morality and discipline, the practice of patience and forbearance as well as that of the four immeasurables[129] are the code of the Saṅgha (monastic order) in accord with the Buddha's teaching, which should on no account give rise to craving and clinging. If there is longing for realizing Buddhahood, achieving bodhi (enlightenment) and so forth, this is like touching fire with one's own hand.

Mañjuśri says, 'If you give rise to the concept of Buddha and Dharma you will only harm yourselves.' Hence, Mañjuśri held up a sword to (meet) Gautama[130] and Aṅgulimālya[131] carried a chopper to Śākyamuni's place (to become his disciple and realize bodhi).

---

dependent, or caused and come into existence only to perish. There are classifications into 2, 3, 5, 6, 7, 11, 13, 16, 18, 20 and 21 categories. So from one voidness arise 12 visible colours and 8 characteristics of form, i.e. $1 + 12 + 8 = 21$.

The 12 visible colours are: blue, yellow, red, white, cloud, smoke, dust, fog, shadow, light, brightness and darkness.

The 8 characteristics of form are: long, short, square, round, high, low, straight and crooked.

129. The four infinite states of the Bodhisattva mind: boundless kindness (maitrī) or bestowing of joy and happiness; boundless compassion (karuṇā) to save from suffering; boundless joy (muditā) on seeing others rescued from suffering; and unrestricted indifference (upekṣā), i.e. rising above these emotions, or relinquishing all things, e.g. distinction of friend and foe, like and dislike, etc.

130. i.e. to kill the objective Gautama, which means that wisdom, symbolized by Mañjuśri, should be used to wipe out the illusion of Buddha who was then called Gautama.

131. Aṅgulimālya: a chaplet of finger-bones which was also the name of a disciple who wore such a chaplet. He was a believer of an Indian sect which taught that nirvāṇa could be won by killing men. After killing 999 persons and using their finger-bones to make a chaplet, he intended to kill his mother, his 1,000th victim. The Buddha took pity on him and converted him to the Dharma. He repented of his crimes, became his disciple and finally realized arhatship.

It is said that when Bodhisattvas (seem to) commit the five unpardonable sins[132] they do not go to the unintermittent hell (avīci) because of their ceaseless perfection (of essence and function and of their use of expedient methods to teach and guide others) and because their's are not the five deadly sins committed by living beings.

All realms from that of wicked demons (pāpīyān) up to that of Buddhas are just filthy grease, and those free from attachments thereto are said to be in the Hīnayāna stage. Then what about those who give rise to disputation about winning or losing and who boast of their ability and understanding? They are quarrelsome monks but not transcendental (wu wei) members of the Sangha (order).

Now if you are free from all desires of and pollution by all that *is* and *is not*, this is the state of the uncreate and is called the right faith. But if you believe in all things, this is unbelief, also called imperfect belief or biased credulity; hence it is called icchantika.[133]

If you want to awaken to and understand (the uncreate) by leaps and bounds, just bury (the duality of) ego and object and when you have cut them off so that they are void, then you can pass through and beyond the three stages of perfection[134] and you are a man above and beyond fate and destiny, who has developed real faith in the Dharma, a Bodhisattva who keeps the rules of morality and discipline (śīla), performs charity (dāna) and realizes wisdom through hearing (the Dharma); who realizes the Bodhisattva-patience (kṣānti) which enables him to give up both the state of Buddha and the condition of living beings, neither observing nor breaking the commandments. Hence it is said that a Bodhisattva neither keeps nor transgresses the precepts.

132. The five deadly sins (pañcānantarya): parricide, matricide, killing an arhat, shedding the blood of a Buddha and destroying the harmony of the Order.

133. Lack of desire for Buddha-enlightenment.

134. See page 96 note 116.

Turbid knowledge (jñāna) purifies itself in (the performance of) its illuminating function to be clear about both pure wisdom (prajñā) and turbid consciousness (vijñāna). This is called the shining wisdom in a Buddha, knowledge in a Bodhisattva, and consciousness in a Hīnayāna man and a living being, which consciousness is also called kleśa (trouble).

Viewed from the Buddha stage it is effect (fruit) derived from cause (seed) and viewed from the worldly realm it is cause (seed) leading to effect (fruit). Viewed from the Buddha stage this is turning the Wheel of the Law (to liberate living beings) and viewed from the worldly plane this is the Wheel of the Law being turned (to hold living beings in bondage).

In the Bodhisattva stage this is called full majesty embellished by precious gems; in the worldly realm it is the grove of five aggregates; and in the Buddha stage it is fundamental ignorance [135] (eventually) enlightened. Hence this (fundamental) ignorance is the corpus or substance of Reality which differs from phenomenal darkness that screens living beings. Hence the former is a subject and the latter an object, that is the former is the subjective hearing and the latter is the objective heard.

That to which you should conform is neither unity nor diversity, neither impermanent nor permanent and neither comes nor goes; it pertains to the vocabulary of living meanings, which is above and beyond the old rut (i.e. dualities, relativities and contraries) for it is neither light nor darkness and neither Buddha nor living being.

Coming and going, impermanence and permanence, and Buddha and living being belong to the vocabulary of dead meanings.

Universality and parochiality, similarity and diversity, and impermanence and permanence belong to the vocabulary of

135. There are two kinds of ignorance: the radical or fundamental, caused by the first thought of self-awareness since the time without beginning; and the phenomenal caused by additional discrimination and conceptions.

heretics. Prajñā-pāramitā is (the self) Buddha-nature and is also called Mahāyāna. Mahā means great and yāna, vehicle. If you hold on to your awareness of your own self, you will become a heretic (who denies the law of causality and holds that things happen spontaneously). So do not cling to anything; just look into (this awareness) for there is no need to search for a Buddha elsewhere. If you seek something else you will become a heretic holding on to cause and condition.

The first patriarch of this land (i.e. Bodhidharma) says, 'If the mind is set on what is right this also implies (its opposite, that is) what is wrong. If you value something you are deluded by it. If you appreciate something, you are deceived by it. Your belief (in something) deceives you and your disbelief (in it) disparages it. Therefore, it is far better to keep from both appreciating and depreciating and from both believing and disbelieving. For the Buddha also is not wu wei (i.e. not non-active) and though he is not non-active, he is not indistinct and inert like empty space. For the Buddha is a broad-minded being who, though vastly experienced in seeing and feeling, is pure and clean (that is disengaged from things seen and felt) and one who cannot be held in bondage by the demon of cupidity and hatred. For the Buddha is above and beyond all bondage and is even free from a speck of desire and grasping, and is also unmindful of this freedom from desire and grasping. For he has achieved the six perfections (pāramitās) and has perfected all modes of salvation. If he wants these to adorn himself, they can provide all forms of adornment, but if he does not want them as adornments, he will not lose any of them. That which contributes to form (good) causality to win blessedness and wisdom and to achieve liberation, is right practice (and training) and is certainly not a weary and burdensome toil which has nothing in common with it.

The three bodies (trikaya: dharmakāya, sambhogakāya and nirmāṇakāya) are (the three manifestations of) the same underlying nature (which shows itself through them).

First, the Dharmakāya is the real Buddha, for the Dharma-kāya Buddha is (non-dual and is) neither light nor darkness because (all dualities such as) light and darkness are just illusions (and have no independent nature of their own). (The word) 'real' is used (here) solely to wipe out that which is 'unreal' but fundamentally the Dharmakāya is beyond all description. To say that the Buddhakāya is non-active and is beyond fate and destiny, and that canopies are offered to him who has attained to supreme enlightenment, are words used to show merely the various progressive stages of attain-ment (but not to describe the Dharmakāya itself).

Therefore, one should begin by (looking into) impurity to bring out purity. Hence the real Buddha body is called the pure and clean Dharmakāya of Vairocana Buddha[136] and is also known (by other names such as) the immaterial Dharma-kāya Buddha, the Great Mirror Wisdom, the (pure) Eighth Consciousness, the Dharmatā[137], the absolute Śūnyatā,[138] the Buddha dwelling in a neither pure nor impure land, the lion in its cave, the wisdom resulting from the diamond-cutter of kleśa, stainless charity, the highest Immaterial Nirvāṇa and the Profound Doctrine. Hence the Third Patriarch (of the Ch'an sect) said:

> If its profoundness you ignore
> You can never practise stillness.[139]

Second, the Sambhogakāya Buddha. When the Buddha realized bodhi under the bo-tree, his body was an illusory

136. Vairocana is the supreme Buddha of the centre.

137. Dharmatā: the underlying nature of all things.

138. Absolute Śūnyatā: the universal, the absolute, complete abstraction without relativity.

139. See *Practical Buddhism* page 35 'Have Faith in Your Mind' lines 5 and 6. (Rider, London; Theosophical Publishing House, Wheaton, Ill., USA).

transformation which is also called (by other names such as) the Buddha-body with excellent physical marks, the Nirmāṇakāya, the perfect reward body of Rocana (Luminating) Buddha, Samatājñāna Buddha,[140] the (Pure) Seventh Consciousness, and the Buddha's Reward Body which is equal to the fifty-two stages of abstract meditation, to Arhatship and Pratyeka-Buddhahood, to all Bodhisattvas who are all subject to sufferings from mortality but are immune against sufferings from the karmic retribution of living beings.

Third, the Nirmāṇakāya Buddha. Now if you are free from craving for and contamination by all things, and also from this idea of freedom from craving and contamination, and if you also keep from the four terms of differentiation[141] all your sayings and your power of speech emanate from the Nirmāṇakāya Buddha who is also called (by other names such as) the countless transformation bodies of Sākyamuni Buddha; the supreme transforming powers of the Buddha; the transcendental potency of the Buddha to roam where he pleases; the Profound Observing Wisdom; the worshipper's Sixth Consciousness purifying the three karmas of body, mouth and mind so that there remains no kleśa to be cut off in the past; there is no self-nature to be preserved in the present and there will be no Buddhahood to be attained in the future, thereby wiping out all the three (periods of) time, in order to empty both the three harmas and three times (of all retribution) so that the three types of dāna[142] are disengaged from all objectives.

A bhikṣu who is passionless when making offerings to the Buddha, purifies all six senses and realizes absolute majesty free from all worldly adornments, for absolute majesty is free from all external pollution and because in it even the Buddha

140. Samatājñāna: the Wisdom of Universal Nature.

141. Differentiation of all things into existence, non-existence, both, neither, or phenomenal, noumenal, both, neither.

142. Three kinds of dāna (charity): Giving of alms, of the Dharma and of fearlessness.

eye cannot be found. When speaking of the practice (of Dharma), the Dharma eye is used to distinguish purity from impurity with, however, no retention of this idea of distinguishing which implies the absence of all objectives including the Dharma eye.

The Mahāratnakūṭa Sūtra says; 'The Dharmakāya cannot be sought by seeing, hearing, feeling and knowing; it cannot be seen by the human eye, for it is formless; it cannot be seen by the deva eye because it is not false; it cannot be seen by the wisdom eye because it is immaterial; it cannot be seen by the Dharma eye, for it is beyond all activities, and it cannot be seen by the Buddha eye, for it is above and beyond all consciousness.'[143]

Not seeing (by means of the five kinds of eye) is Buddha seeing which, though of the same underlying nature of form, is devoid of the characteristics of form – hence it is the (absolute) form of reality; and though of the same nature of the void, it is not empty like space – hence it is the (absolute) voidness of reality.

Form and voidness are terms used to indicate an illness and its remedy. The (text on the) meditation on the Dharmadhātu (Fa chia kuan)[144] says, 'Neither form nor formlessness, and neither voidness nor its opposite, can be spoken of.' When the eyes, ears, nose, tongue, body and intellect are unresponsive to both what *is* and *is not*, this is called entry into the

143. The five kinds of eye: the human eye that sees all things as real; the deva eye, divine eye or unlimited vision; the wisdom eye that sees all things as unreal; the Dharma eye that penetrates all things, to see the truth that releases us from reincarnation; and the Buddha eye, the eye of the enlightened one who sees all and is omniscient.
144. A method of meditation leading to awakening to the Dharmadhātu as taught in the Avataṁsaka Sūtra. The Chinese patriarch of the Avatamsaka school, Tu Shun, (died A.D. 640) teaches this meditation in three phases: first on absolute voidness of the noumenon; second, on unimpeded interrelation of noumenon and phenomenon; and third, on all-embracing universal illumination (in regard to the real in contrast to the seeming).

seventh stage (of Bodhisattva development into Buddha-hood). Those who have passed through the first seven stages do not retrograde[145] but those in the three higher stages whose mind-grounds are clean can be easily polluted; hence they feel scorched at the mere talk of fire.

Above the realm of form, charity (dāna) is an illness and greediness is its healing remedy (but) below the realm of form, greediness is an illness and charity its healing medicine.[146]

Discipline (śīla) is fulfilled by cutting off all worldly habits externally, that is by moral action of body and mouth or internally by the moral character of the mind,[147] the latter being called hidden or passionless discipline.

Even a mere stir of the mind or a rising thought breaks the commandments. Now if you are not disturbed by what *is* and what *is not* under all circumstances, if you also do not dwell in this freedom from disturbance and are again unmindful of this non-dwelling, this is your quest for All-knowledge, also called the diligent preservation or wide-spread circulation of this all-pervading knowledge.

(The state) before awakening and understanding is called mother and (the state) after awakening is called son. Non-

145. Of the ten stages of Bodhisattva development, the seventh stage can easily slip into the void because of its deep meditation on voidness wherein there is neither Bodhi to be sought nor living beings to liberate. Because of this voidness, the meditator experiences difficulty in continuing his practice. Hence he should give rise to the idea of Bodhi and living beings to enter the eighth stage of imperturbability in order to realize the Buddha-fruit. See *The Śūraṅgama Sūtra* page 172, the ten highest stages of Bodhisattva attainment (daśabhūmi). (Rider, London).

146. Above the world of form is the formless or immaterial realm where charity is wrong because it is no longer needed by those already disengaged from desire for material gains. Since they have slipped into voidness, they should get out of inaction by giving rise to greediness which can be easily wiped out in the eighth stage of imperturbability. Below the world of form is the realm of desire where greediness is a handicap and should be wiped out by cultivating charity.

147. i.e. external moral action in contrast with inner moral character.

clinging to both states with unmindfulness of them result in
the death of both mother and son, which means freedom
from bondage to good and evil, to Buddhas and living beings,
and to all measuring and figuring. Hence it is said that the
Buddha is a man who is beyond all bondage and above all
measure. The desire of knowledge and understanding of the
profound meanings (of the sūtras) is like a mother who loves
her son and gives him much butter without even knowing
if he can digest it.

This is the trouble (kleśa) in the ten stages of Bodhisattva
development caused by the reverence and admiration which
men and devas have for them; in the worlds of form and
beyond form where serenity (dhyāna) and bliss hinder the
realization of transcendental powers to fly either visibly or
invisibly to all Buddha-lands in the ten directions for listening
to the Dharma expounded there; in the causal practice of (the
four immeasurables): kindness (maitrī), compassion (karuṇā),
joy (muditā) and indifference (upekṣā); in the causal study of
the immaterial and universal 'mean'; in the causal realization
of the three insights,[148] six supernatural powers[149] and four
unhindered powers of interpretation;[150] in the development
of the Mahāyāna mind to perfect the four universal vows;[151]

148. 1, insight into the mortal conditions of self and others in previous
lives; 2, into future mortal conditions; and 3, into present mortal sufferings
to put an end to all passions and their consequences.

149. Ṣaḍabhijñā: 1, divine sight; 2, divine hearing; 3, knowledge of the
minds of all living beings; 4, knowledge of all forms of previous existence
of self and others; 5, power to appear at will in any place and to have
absolute freedom; and 6, insight into the ending of the stream of birth
and death.

150. Pratisaṃvid, the four unhindered or unlimited Bodhisattva
powers of interpretation, or reasoning, i.e. in the Dharma, the letter of the
Law; artha, its meaning; nirukti, in any language, or form of expression;
and pratibhāna, in eloquence, or argument.

151. To save all living beings without limit; to put an end to all kleśa
however numerous; to study and practise endless Dharma-doors to
enlightenment; and to realize Supreme enlightenment.

in the initial, second, third and fourth stages of Bodhisattva development (into Buddhahood) due to clear explanations (involving expectation of results); in the fifth, sixth and seventh stages due to (fixed) views; in the eighth, ninth and tenth stages due to dual views of noumenon and phenomenon; and in countless aeons of study (to realize) the Buddha-fruit. All this is because of the eagerness to acquire knowledge from profound sentences (in the sūtras) without appreciating that they are precisely hindering passions. Hence it is said that the current of (wrong) views drifts the Fragrant Elephant[152] about aimlessly.

*

Question (by a monk). 'Do you see things'?

Answer (by the master). 'Yes, I do.'

Question. 'What next after this seeing'?

Answer. 'Seeing is non-dual.'

Question. 'If seeing is non-dual, there should be no seeing that (precedes and) perceives the following seeing'.

Answer. 'If there be further seeing after the first one, which one is right? This is (explained) in the following sentence; When absolute seeing perceives the essence of seeing (ālaya), the former is not the latter which still differs from it; how then can false seeing (by the eyes) attain that absolute seeing?'[153]

Hence one should refrain from seeing, hearing and feeling the Dharma thereby ensuring a ready prophesy by all Buddhas of one's forthcoming realization of bodhi.

Question. 'If seeing is irrelevant to the Buddha's prophecy, what is the use of prophesying?'

Answer. 'The aim of our sect is primarily to awaken students by freeing them from all that *is* and that *is not*, just

152. A Bodhisattva.
153. Cf *Śūraṅgama Sūtra* page 47. (Rider, London).

like washing dirty clothes. Hence it is said; Keeping from all forms is the Buddha stage and throwing away both reality and unreality so that the solitary "Mean" deepens and further deepens, is to reach the correct path and then to continue advancing until it tallies with the right degree by itself, which is what "prophecy" means'.

Ignorance is father, love is mother, and self is illness and is also that medicine which cures all diseases, and that knife which kills ignorance and love, or the father and mother respectively. Hence the killing of father and the injuring of mother are similes of the wiping out of all dharmas (things). Likewise the habit of eating out of regulation hours[154] should be discontinued, for holding on to things that *are* and *are not* is just this eating out of regulation hours which is an evil, is like unclean food put in a precious vessel, is breaking the commandments, is a pack of lies and leads to confusion.

A Buddha is a man who seeks nothing. If you now search for what *is* and what *is not*, whatever you gain and whatever you do runs counter to and vilifies this Buddha. A taint of desire is a giver of prophecy. Now if you are free from desire, do not dwell in this freedom from desire, and if you are also unmindful of this non-dwelling, this is the fire of prajñā (wisdom) which burns the fingers of the giver of prophecy; this is regardlessness for one's body and life, mutilation of the body,[155] retiring from the world and throwing this world to another place elsewhere. But if there remains in your body even a tiny speck of the teaching from the twelve divisions of the Mahāyāna canon, or an atom of what *is* and what *is not*, this is to remain captive in the net (of delusion). For where there is search and gain, and where the mind stirs and thought arises, there is the predicament of all jackals.

154. i.e. eating after noon which is forbidden in all monasteries.

155. To which the Buddha was subjected in a former life. Cf *Ch'an and Zen Teaching, First Series,* The Diamond Cutter of Doubts, page 182 (Rider, London; Shambala, Berkeley).

He who seeks nothing and wins nothing is a great bestower (of the Dharma) and can give the lion's roar;[156] he does not dwell in this state of gainlessness and also does not hold on to this concept of non-dwelling. He is called a lion (i.e. a fearless man) who has cut off all six senses; for whom there is neither selfness nor otherness; who is free from all devils; can put Mount Sumeru in a mustard seed; is free from desire, anger and the eight winds,[157] and can suck up in his mouth all the water of the four oceans; who is unresponsive to all baseless words and speeches which cannot enter his ears, and who prevents all evils arising in his body that are harmful to others by confining all fires (of passions) in his own belly.

Now in every circumstance if he is free from delusion, disturbance, anger and joy which he can banish completely from all six sense organs, he is an unconcerned man surpassing (others in) knowledge, interpretation, austerity and devotion. This is called the deva eye (divine eye) or perfect sight; the underlying nature of the dharma-realm; the making of a vehicle to drive away all causes and effects; and the Buddha appearing in the world to liberate living beings.

So if the preceding thought does not arise, there will be no following thought to succeed it. If the karma of the preceding thought withers, this is delivering living beings. If the preceding thought is one of anger, it should be cured by its medicine (that is) joy, which means the Buddha delivering living beings.

Therefore, all teaching words are like medicines that cure illnesses. Since illnesses differ from one another their remedies vary. Consequently the Buddha is spoken of sometimes as existing sometimes as non-existent. Discussion of reality aims at healing illnesses. So every word corresponds to reality if the illness is cured but is false if the disease is not

156. The lion's roar which subdues devils, conquers heretics and destroys all passions.
157. The eight winds, or influences that fan the passions, i.e. gain, loss, defamation, eulogy, praise, ridicule, sorrow and joy.

cured. True words become false if they lead to (perverse) views and false words become true if they prevent perversion. So illnesses stand for falsehood which can be healed by their corresponding remedies.

Teachings such as 'The Buddha appears in the world to deliver living beings' in nine of the Mahāyāna's twelve classes of sūtras[158] are a partial revelation (of the whole truth adapted to the capability of the hearers). (But) anger and joy as well as illnesses and (healing) remedies come from oneself and do not belong to somebody else. Where does the Buddha appear in the world? Where are living beings being liberated? This is what the (Diamond) Sūtra means by 'it is true that not a living being is led to the extinction of reincarnation.'[159]

It is also said that no desire of Buddha–bodhi and no craving for both what *is* and *is not* mean the liberation of others, and that disengagement from oneself is self-liberation. Since ailments differ from one another, their healing remedies also vary. Therefore, one should not rely on such things as Buddha, Bodhi, etc. which are but bondage. This is why no wise men fix their minds in one direction.

In the teaching school discussions and examples are just yellow leaves and empty fists to deceive children. If you do not know the ideas behind all this, you are unenlightened. It is said that a Bodhisattva developing wisdom (prajñā) should

158. The nine kinds of Mahāyāna sūtras are: 1, the Buddha sermons (sūtras); 2, metrical pieces (geyas); 3, prophecies (vyākaraṇas); 4, chants or poems (gāthās); 5, impromptu or unsolicited addresses (udānas); 6, narratives (ityuktas or itivṛttakas; 7, stories of former lives of the Buddha (jātakas); 8, expanded sūtras (vaipulyas); and 9, miracles, etc. (adbhuta-dharmas).

The twelve kinds of Mahāyāna sūtras are the above nine to which are added: 10, sūtras expounded because of a request or query; or because certain precepts were violated; or because of certain events (nidānas); 11, parables (avadānas); and 12, general treatises (upadeśa).

159. Cf *Ch'an and Zen Teaching, First Series*, part III, The Diamond Cutter of Doubts, page 161, third para. (Rider, London; Shambala, Berkeley).

not cling to the Buddha's words and to the precepts which compare anger to a rock and desire to river water. Now if you can only free yourselves from anger and desire, you will pass through mountains, cross rivers and penetrate stone walls; this is like curing worldlings suffering from deafness. As to those who are listeners and glib talkers, it is like curing defective sight by teaching them that all stages from manhood up to Buddha-hood are gains and that all those from manhood down to hells are losses; in order to define what is right and what is wrong. Hence the Third Patriarch said:

> Gain and loss, and right and wrong
> Should be laid down now at once.[160]

For grasping neither what *is* nor what *is not* is non-dwelling in causal states, and if this is additionally free from this idea of non-dwelling, it is called non-dwelling in the patient endurance (kṣanti) of the void (a state attained by regarding both the phenomenal and the noumenal as unreal and void.[161]

160. Cf *Practical Buddhism*, Part II, Have faith in your Mind, page 37. (Rider, London; The Theosophical Publishing House, Wheaton, USA)

161. Kṣanti or patient endurance in (a) adverse circumstances and (b) in spiritual states. There are groups of 2, 3, 4, 5, 6, 10 and 14, indicating various forms of patience, equanimity, forbearance, endurance, constancy, or 'perseverance of the Bodhisattvas' both in mundane and spiritual things. Below are the common groups:

The 2 kinds of patient endurance of: (a) the attitude of all living beings who should on no account become the objects of our anger, resentment and retaliation even for their insults and assaults; (b) non-rising thought in order to realize the uncreate.

These two kinds of patient endurance are also attained by: (a) being indifferent to praise, respect and offerings by others as well as to their censure, insults and assaults; (b) being unperturbed by material states such as heat, cold, gale, rain, thirst, hunger, old age, illness, death, etc. and by mental states such as anger, hate, sorrow, sadness, etc.

The ten kinds of patient endurance:

1, of sounds and echoes. Those reborn in the Paradise of the Bliss hear the seven jewelled trees proclaim the Three Treasures (Buddha, Dharma and Saṅgha) thereby realizing the patient endurance of 1, sound and voice;

He who regards himself as a Buddha and thinks he understands the Ch'an path, clings to the inner (wrong) view and he whose practice and rralization are based on causes and conditions, grasps the outer (wrong) view. Hence (Ch'an master) Pao Chih said, 'Both inner and outer views are wrong.' For he whose eyes, ears, nose and tongue are immune against pollution by desire of what *is* and what *is not*, is really (qualified to) receive and keep a four-line gāthā,[162] and also attains to the four stages of (Hīnayāna) saintship,[163] for his

---

2, of meekness and submissiveness; and 3, of non-creativeness, or of the uncreate.

When hearing the sounds of trees, they awaken to the doctrine of non-existing (noumenal) yet existent (phenomenal) things.

2, of meekness and submissiveness. Their minds are meek to the Dharma; their wisdom agrees with reality.

3, of the uncreate which agrees with absolute reality.

4, of illusions which show that all things owe their seeming existence to causes and conditions which have no independent nature of their own.

5, of flames which is likened to all states having no independent nature of their own.

6, of dreams which likens the non-existent mind to dreams which are unreal.

7, of echoes which show that word, speech, voice and sound come from the union of causes and conditions like an echo in the valley that has no independent nature of its own.

8, of shadows which show that the body is formed by five aggregates which have no independent nature of their own.

9, of transformations which show that all things fundamentally non-existent, suddenly appear and suddenly vanish because they have no independent nature of their own.

10, of the void which shows that both phenomenal and noumenal things are unreal like space which is formless. This is what the text means.

162. A Buddhist term meaning the student is qualified to receive and practise the Dharma in any gāthā. Cf Ch'an and Zen Teaching, first series, The Diamond Cutter of Doubts, page 169. (Rider, London; Shambala, Berkeley)

163. Four phala or grades of saintship: śrota-āpanna-phala, sakṛ-dāgāmi-phala, anāgāmi-phala and arhat-phala or four stages of Hīnayāna attainment.

sense organs are devoid of objects, which means his realization of six supernatural powers.[164]

Now if you are not conditioned by what *is* and *is not*, if you do not dwell in this freedom from such conditions, and if you are further unmindful of this concept of freedom, this is your realization of supernatural powers. If you further do not hold on to these supernatural powers, you will be free from attachment to them; and a Bodhisattva free from this concept of supernatural powers, leaves no traces, and is a Buddha, an upward and a most inconceivable man of supreme heaven[165] and of radiating wisdom.

Praise causes joy which is an objective state and stands for (supreme) heaven. Praised is the man and when he and his heaven confront and unite with each other, there will result pure wisdom which is heaven (nirvāṇa) and correct wisdom which is the man.

For originally man is not Buddha, and calling him a Buddha will result in bodily bondage. Now if you are free from the concept of the realization of Buddhahood and if you also keep from this freedom from such a concept, this is wiping out that bondage and is called absolute thatness (bhūtatathatā or chen ju in Chinese) or the substance of suchness.

The quest for Buddhahood and that for enlightenment are but manifestations of body and mind. For all desires expose the body and mind. If you seek bodhi (enlightenment) though your quest is unsurpassed, it will increase your passion-karma (which hinders your mind). For your quest for Buddhahood will land you in (the illusory realm of) Buddha-beings. Your quest for all that *is* and that *is not* will land you in (the realm of) sentient beings. Now if you only look (at things) without differentiating between what *is* and what *is not*, you will not slip into fate and destiny. Now if you are indifferent to all

164. See page 107 note 149.
165. A Buddhist term for Nirvāṇa.

sound, smell, taste, touch and dharma (things) and do not cling to all objective states, if your mind is free from all impurities, this is the enlightening cause (liao yin) of your realization of Buddhahood.[166] If you study the scriptures and seek their interpretation, this is the causal realization of Buddhahood. It is correct to say that you see and know the Buddha but you will slander him if you say that he possesses the faculty of knowing and of seeing. It is correct to say that the Buddha knows, sees, hears and speaks. This is like saying that fire is seen, which is correct but it is wrong to say that fire sees. This is like saying that the knife cuts objects, which is correct but it is wrong to say that objects cut the knife. Those who know, see, hear and speak of the Buddha are as many as there are sand grains in the Ganges. But among myriads of people there is not one who is the knowing, seeing, hearing and speaking Buddha. This is because they lack the eye (of wisdom) and rely on others to see; the teaching school calls it knowledge by comparison and inference.[167]

Now the quest for Buddha-knowledge also pertains to knowledge by comparison and inference. All worldly examples are concordant[168] illustrations. The incomplete teaching (of Hīnayāna) is (wholly) concordant examplification. The complete teaching (of Mahāyāna) is discordant exemplification. The sacrifice of head, eyes, marrow and brain belongs to discordant illustration.

The relinquishment of (exalted) things such as Buddha-hood, bodhi, etc. pertains to discordant illustration. Things

166. The three causes of Buddhahood: (a) the direct cause, associated with the seed of Buddha-nature inherent in us; (b) the enlightening cause, associated with the functioning of Buddha-wisdom (prajñā) inherent in us; and (c) the environing cause, associated with practice and training which results in the stage of Buddhahood.

167. i.e. comparison of the known and inference of the unknown, e.g. inference of fire from smoke.

168. Which agree with the worldly way of life.

most difficult to forego are likened to head, eyes, marrow and brain. If there is attachment to what *is* and what *is not*, this is the head disturbed and confused by these states. But before confronting these external states, they are only marrow and brain.

Being on the saintly plane, the Buddha familiarizes himself with the worldly way of life to mix with living beings in order to befriend and convert them. He endures the same kind of suffering as the hungry ghosts whose limbs are scorched by fire (in the hells) in order to teach them prajñā-pāramitā so that they can develop a mind set on it. If he stayed on his original saintly plane how could he go and speak to them?

The Buddha enters the realms of all species of beings to act as a raft (that leads them from the sea of suffering to the other shore of bodhi) but he endures with them untold hardships and sufferings. So he enters the worlds of misery and also endures the same sufferings of all living beings, the only difference being that unlike them he is free to stay or leave. The Buddha is not empty space; then how can he escape from suffering? If you say he does not suffer, this is irresponsible and commonplace talk. Do not talk nonsense and say that supernatural powers give the Buddha comfortable sovereignty or not. Moreover, he who keeps the rules of discipline, dares not say the Buddha is either wordly or saintly and is independent or not; besides praising the Buddha's medicine (that cures the illness of ignorance) he always avoids giving rise to the ugly duality of two extremes.

According to the teaching, he who sets up the Buddha-bodhi formulates a state which is one extreme (of a duality) thereby committing a grave mistake. It also says that he who speaks of this to a non-buddhist is not wrong because it is like the spiritual milk which can cure all worldly illnesses. This cow stays neither on high grounds nor in marshes, hence its milk can be used as a medicine. (Here) high grounds stand for the state of Buddha and marshes for that of living beings.

To say that the Tathāgata's enlightened Dharmakāya is free from all illnesses, that his power of speech is unobstructed, that his ascension is supreme, and that he is beyond and above birth and death, is on the side of light. To speak of birth, old age, illness and death, with consequential intolerable suffering, is on the side of darkness. Contracting dysentery after taking mushroom soup is (like) darkness that envelops light.

Now you have only to forsake both light and darkness, the idea of forsaking them and also that which is neither light nor darkness.

Hearers (śrāvakas) and heretics give rise to discrimination about the birth of the Buddha in a palace, his taking a wife called Yaśodharā[169] and the eight aspects of his life.[170] They contend that the Buddha's Dharmakāya is not the human body that requires food to live and even Cunda said, 'I know the Tathāgata does not actually receive and eat my offering of food.'[171]

It is most important to have the two eyes (of wisdom) to look into and wipe out the two extremes of all dualities. Do not be content with only one eye to direct it to one side (of a duality). For if you direct it to the side of Mahāśrī, a giver of weal, this implies its opposite, that is the side of Kālarātri, the giver of woe (for weal and woe alternate with each other).

169. Yaśodharā: wife of the Buddha and mother of Rāhula, who became a nun after her husband's enlightenment. According to the Lotus Sūtra, she is to become the Buddha Raśmi–śata–sahasra–paripūrṇa–dhvaja.

170. The eight aspects of the Buddha's life: 1, descent into and abode in the Tuṣita heaven; 2, entry into his mother's womb; 3, abode there visibly preaching to the devas; 4, birth from his mother's side in Lumbinī; 5, leaving home at 19 or 25 as a hermit; 6, after six years' suffering attaining enlightenment; 7, turning the wheel of the Law or preaching; and 8, at 80 entering Nirvāṇa.

171. Quote from the Mahāparinirvāṇa Sūtra, part 2, which relates that Cunda supplied the Buddha with his last meal which he purposely accepted to comfort the whole assembly.

A wise host who met these two guests would reject and leap over both.[172]

Now if your mind can be (made) empty like space, your practice will be successful. In the West (i.e. India) our great-great-grand-father (the Buddha) compared the immaculate vast Snowy mountains (the Himālayas) to the Great Nirvāṇa. The First Patriarch of China (Bodhidharma) said. 'The mind should be (insensate) like wood and stone.' The Third Patriarch said, 'Profound is this state of suchness – Lofty and beyond illusions.' Hui Neng said, 'Don't think of either good or evil.' My late master (Ma Tsu) said, 'Like one losing his way who does not even know the direction he takes.' Seng Chao said, 'Obstruct your knowledge and block your intelligence to ensure the intuitive recognition (of reality) in solitude.' Mañjuśrī said, 'His mind is (vast) like the great emptiness, hence I salute Him who looks into nothing – which is a profound sūtra which can be neither heard nor practised.'

Now all that *is* and that *is not* should be neither seen nor heard in order to block all six sense organs. If you can do so, you will be qualified to study and practise the sūtras. If these true words, unpleasant to the ear and bitter to the tongue, can be listened to until your second and third transmigrations, you will be able to proceed to where there are no Buddhas to sit on a great bodhimaṇḍala to reveal your attainment of supreme enlightenment, transforming evil into good and good into evil; using evil Dharmas to teach and convert all Bodhisattvas of the ten stages and using good Dharmas to teach and convert the hells and hungry ghosts so that they can proceed to where there is light to untie bonds caused by (attachment to) light and to where there is darkness to untie bonds caused by (clinging to) darkness; transmitting gold into earth and earth into gold, thus making all sorts of transformations at will. Then when someone beseeches help and salvation from somewhere separated from this earth by

172. See the Mahāparinirvāṇa Sūtra, chapter 12.

countless worlds as many as there sand grains in the Ganges, the Bhagavat will appear with all his thirty-two perfect physical marks in front of the supplicant to expound the Dharma to him in his own language. In response to different potentialities he will appear in many transformation bodies according to their fates and destinies.

Keeping from the (duality of) subject and object in the world still pertains to the (objective) other shore (of Nirvāṇa) which is a restrictive form of functioning.[173] In the Buddha-work of salvation, by universal form of functioning is meant (something like) a great body hidden in formlessness, and a loud voice inherent in silence; for instance, the fire imminent in (a piece of) wood and the sound innate in a bell and a drum.

When propitious cause and condition are not prevalent for the manifestation of this (absolute) functioning, it cannot be reckoned what as *is* or *is not*. The side-lined reward (i.e. the good side of a duality) ensures a rebirth in the realm of devas which is worthless like tears and snot.

The Bodhisattva's six perfections (pāramitā) and myriad lines of excellent conduct are like riding dead bodies to the other shore or like escaping from a prison through an opening in its latrine.

The Buddhas thirty-two excellent physical marks are compared to a greasy and dirty robe. There is no such thing as a Buddha unaffected by the five aggregates; if he is not empty like space how can he be unaffected by them? The Buddha differs from living beings in that he is free to stay or leave anywhere he likes, and can go from one realm of devas to another deva realm and from one Buddha-land to another in his usual fashion.

It is also said that according to the Triyāna teaching, when a Bodhisattva has received donations from the faithful and when the latter suffer in the realm of hells, he should have

173. i.e. subtle attachment to Nirvāṇa.

kindness and compassion for them and appear as one of them to convert and guide them in repayment of his indebtedness instead of staying in Nirvāṇa (to enjoy himself).

It is also said that when you confront fire, if you do not touch it with your hand, it will not burn you. Now if you are free from the ten impure minds (set on) desire, love, infection, hatred, clinging, abiding, dependence, settling, grasping and fondness, and if you can subject each of them to the threefold elimination (technique)[174] and thus leap over and beyond all of them, you can see into them and make use of them in the performance of your prajñā (wisdom) at will, thereby changing all your behaviour, activity, speech, silence, crying and laughing into Buddha-vision.

174. By keeping from these polluted minds, from the idea of so keeping away and from the awareness thereof. See also page 76 fourth paragraph.

The Fourth Generation After The Patriarch Hui Neng: Ch'an Master Huang Po, Also Called Hsi Yun and Tuan Chi

MASTER Huang Po was a native of Fu Chou (capital of Fu Chien province). When he arrived at Lo Yang for the first time, he begged for food (in the street) grumbling, 'Please give one more bowl.'

An old woman came out of her retreat, saying 'What an insatiate man!' The master retorted, 'You have not given me rice, how can you blame me for being insatiate?'

The old woman laughed and shut the door. The master found her unusual and asked to see her. During their conversation he heard her words which revealed (the truth). After a while he took leave of the old woman who said, 'You should go to Nan Chang to call on the great master Ma (Tsu).'

When the master arrived at Nan Chang, Ma Tsu had passed away. Hearing that Ma Tsu's stūpa was erected at the stone gate (of Nan Chang) he went there to pay reverence to the great master. At the time Ch'an master Ta Chi of Pai Chang (monastery) was staying in a hut by the side of the stūpa, and Huang Po (on seeing him) told him of his first intention to call on Ma Tsu and of his wish to hear about the impact of the great master's (revealing) words.

Pai Chang asked, 'Where does the eminent and dignified one come from?'[1]

1. Pai Chang posed this question to see if Huang Po knew anything about his own mind that had ordered him to come to the stūpa.

Huang Po replied, 'The eminent and dignified one comes from Ling Nan (i.e. Kuang Tung province).'

Pai Chang asked, 'What is the purpose of the eminent and dignified one's visit?'

Huang Po replied, 'The purpose of the eminent and dignified one's visit is not for anything else.' He then knelt down to pay reverence to Pai Chang.

Pai Chang then related the story of his second visit to Ma Tsu during which while he was standing by his side, the great master Ma looked at the dust-whisk hanging on his bed (stead). He continued, 'I asked the great master, "Is it precisely this functioning (yung) which should be kept away?" The great master asked, "Later what will you do when you move the two pieces of skin[2] to receive others?" I took the dust-whisk which I held up, and the great master said, "It is precisely this functioning which should be kept away."[3] I then hung the whisk back in its previous place. Thereat the great master gave a loud shout which made me deaf for three (successive) days.'[4]

When Huang Po heard this, he put out his tongue (in astonishment).

2. A Ch'an idiom which means the two lips or the mouth that talks to callers.

3. This is known as Ma Tsu's technique of 'ta chi ta yung' (lit. great in function and great in potentiality) which consists of using the master's strong functioning or the power of his absolute mind to awaken the great potentiality of a disciple so that the latter can absorb the truth. This can be done only when an enlightened master meets a student of exceptionally high spirituality.

When using this absolute functioning to awaken a disciple, this functioning should not be clung to in order to avoid the duality of subject and object, hence 'This is precisely this functioning which should be kept away.'

The word 'It is precisely this functioning' are spoken while the dust-whisk is being held up, and the words 'which should be kept away' are spoken when the dust-whisk is being hung back in its original place.

4. The digit 3 in 'three days' stands for the three karmic conditions of body, mouth and mind. Pai Chang meant that Ma Tsu's loud shout i.e.

Pai Chang asked, 'Will you be a successor to the great master Ma?'

Huang Po replied, 'No, it is only to-day that I have heard from you about the great master Ma's (technique of) great functioning in response to a great potentiality. Moreover, I did not meet him before. If I succeeded to him, I would bring about the destruction of my (Dharma-) descendants.'[5]

Pai Chang said, 'If your competence equals that of your master, you will reduce his merits by one half; you seem to surpass your master in functioning.'

*

(One day) Pai Chang asked Huang Po, 'Where do you come from?'

Huang Po replied, 'From the foot of Ta Hsiung mountain where I went to pick mushrooms.'

Pai Chang asked, 'Did you see the great worm?'[6]

Thereat, Huang Po gave a tiger's roar and Pai Chang picked up a hatchet threatening to attack Huang Po who then gave him a slap in the face.[7]

Pai Chang giggled and returned to the abbot's room.

(That evening) in the meeting hall Pai Chang said, 'There is a tiger at the foot of Ta Hsiung mountain; you all should see it. To-day I have been bitten by it.'

*

(One day) as the community went out to open up new land,

his great functioning, suddenly liberated him from the three karmas of deed, word and thought which no longer held him in bondage. The digit 3 also means sense organs, sense data and consciousnesses which are disconnected.

5. A succession from an unknown master will not benefit one's own disciples for lack of a spiritual link from master to pupils.

6. Tigers were called great worms in China in the old days.

7. This explains why later Lin Chi slapped the face of his master Huang Po in continued use of the great functioning technique. Cf *Ch'an and Zen Teaching, Second Series*, page 86. (Rider, London; Shambala, Berkeley).

Pai Chang said to Huang Po, 'Venerable Ācārya,[8] it is not easy to open up waste land.'

Huang Po replied, 'I just follow others to work.'

Pai Chang said, 'Please speak of functioning.'

Huang Po replied, 'How dare I shirk responsibility?'

Pai Chang asked, 'How much land have you opened up?'

Huang Po hit the ground thrice with his mattock. Thereat Pai Chang gave a loud shout and Huang Po shut his ears and withdrew.

*

Nan Ch'uan one day asked Huang Po, 'Who lives in a citadel made of gold with silver walls?'

Huang Po replied, 'The abode of holy men.'

Nan Ch'uan asked, 'There is another man, what is his place of abode?'[9]

Huang Po went near Nan Ch'uan, brought his palms together and stood still.

Nan Ch'uan said, 'If you cannot say who, why don't you ask the old teacher Wang?'[10]

Huang Po then asked (the same question:) 'There is another man, what is his place of abode?'

Nan Ch'uan replied, 'What a pity!'[11]

*

(One day) the master went to the meeting hall, and as soon

8. Ācārya: a teacher, instructor.

9. This refers to the mind inherent in man.

10. Nan Ch'uan's lay surname was Wang and as he liked to joke, he called himself 'Old teacher Wang'. This is probably the origin of the present title given in Japan to Zen masters who are called 'Roshi' or 'old teacher'.

11. Huang Po gave the correct answer because the acts of going near Nan Ch'uan, of bringing his palms together and of standing still revealed the functioning of the mind.

The literal meaning is, 'It would be a pity if there were another man beside the above one as revealed by his functioning because this extra man

124

as the monks had gathered there, he took a staff to hit and disperse them. He then called them and when they turned back their heads, he said, 'The crescent is like a bent bow, very little rain but only strong winds.'[12]

*

One day the master clenched his (right) fist and said to the assembly, 'The monks all over the country are here (in my fist). If I venture to speak of this you are all at sixes and sevens. If I do not venture to speak of this, it is not worth a clenched fist.'

A monk asked the master, 'What is it if you venture to speak of it?'

The master replied, 'All at sixes and sevens.'

The monk asked, 'What is it when you do not venture to speak of it?'

The master replied, 'Everywhere.'

*

One day chancellor P'ei Hsiu invited the master to his official residence and showed him his notes on his understanding (of the Transmission).

The master received the notes and put them on a seat without even looking at them. After a long while, he asked the chancellor, 'Do you understand?'

P'ei Hsiu replied, 'It is unfathomable.'

---

would be an illusion'. The living meaning is the mind the functioning of which spoke these three words.

The above dialogue should not be interpreted literally for the gist of it is to reveal the mind by means of its functioning which all students of The Transmission outside the Teaching should realize in order to leap over the realm of illusion and suffering.

Readers should refer to the technical terms *T'i yung* – substance and function – fully explained in my book *Ch'an and Zen Teaching, Second Series*, page 62. (Rider, London; Shambala, Berkeley).

12. The winds stand for stirs in the mind which give no result i.e. the rain or the realization of self-nature and attainment of Buddhahood.

The master said, 'If you so understand it is worth something but if you express it in ink and on paper, where then is our sect?'

P'ei Hsiu then presented the following poem to the master:

Since a Bodhisattva has once transmitted the mind-seal to you,
With a pearl in the forehead of your seven foot body
You have stayed for ten years in Szu Chuen province.
Today you have sailed to the coast of Chang Chou
Followed in your high footsteps by a thousand elephants
     and dragons
Who have come from very far away to form a propitious cause
By offering to serve as your disciples
But knowing not who your successor will be.

The master was, however, not elated by this gāthā that praised him but from then on the House of Huang Po prospered in the region south of the Yang Tse river.

*

(One day) a monk asked the master, 'What is Tao and how is it practised?'

The master asked back, 'What Tao do you want to practise?'

The monk said, 'If so what is the purpose of Ch'an training and of the study of the Tao handed down from master to master of the Ch'an sect?'

The master replied, 'All this is to receive and guide men of dull roots and is not reliable.'

The monk asked, 'If this is to receive and guide men of dull roots, what will you teach to men of superior roots?'

The master replied, 'If they are men of superior roots, what can you teach them to (help them) seek their own selves. If their own selves cannot be found, what is the Dharma which can match this (state)? Have you not read this in the sūtra, "What do the Dharmas look like?"'

The monk said, 'If so, there is no need to seek anything.'

The master said, 'You can thus save your strength.'

The monk said, 'If so, this is almost complete annihilation but does not show (its) non-existence.'

The master asked, 'Who teaches its non-existence? What is it you want to seek?'

The monk asked back, 'If you do not formulate the search for it, why do you say it should not be annihilated?'

The master replied, 'If you do not search for it, that is all; who teaches you its annihilation? You see (empty) space before you; how are you going to annihilate it?'

The monk asked, 'Is this Dharma identical with space?'

The master replied, 'Does space tell you day and night whether it is identical or different? As soon as I speak of it you immediately give rise to your (discriminative) interpretation.'

The monk asked, 'Do you even forbid interpretation?'

The master replied, 'I have never hindered you. Besides interpretation pertains to feeling and feeling screens wisdom.'

The monk asked, 'Is it correct that no feelings should arise?'

The master asked back, 'If no feelings arise, who says it is correct?'

The monk said, 'As soon as I speak, (you seem to) call it a slip of the tongue.'

The master asked, 'The truth is that you do not understand my words; what slip do you mean?'

The monk said, 'So far all your words are to contradict others but you have not taught the real Dharma.'

The master asked, 'The real Dharma is not upside-down but your questions give rise to inversion. What real Dharma do you search for?'

The monk asked, 'If my questions give rise to inversion, what about your answers to them?'

The master said, 'Just look into things that concern yourself but be unconcerned about other people's.' He added, 'This is like a mad dog barking when there is motion without even distinguishing between the wind in the grass and that among the trees.'

He further said, 'This Ch'an sect of mine, inherited from past generations, has never taught people to seek knowledge and interpretation. It formulates the study of Tao only to receive and guide beginners, but in reality Tao cannot be learned, for the study of it (is a passion that) screens the Tao. Tao has neither direction nor location, and is called the Mahāyāna-mind. This mind is neither within nor without nor in-between, and is beyond direction and location. The most important thing is to avoid knowing and interpreting. It is only said that the capacity of passion is where the Tao lies, and when this capacity is exhausted the mind is beyond direction and location. This Tao is the Bhūtatathatā and is nameless. Worldly men do not understand this and deceive themselves by staying in the midst of passions.

This is why the Buddha appeared in the world to bare this matter. In case people do not understand it, it is expediently called Tao but you should not cling to (the word) Tao thereby giving rise to interpretation. Hence the saying, 'When the fish is caught, forget all about the trap' and then your body and mind will attain to the Tao of themselves.

He who knows his mind and reaches its source is called a śramaṇa.[13] The śramaṇa-fruit results from quieting passions but not from study. Now if you use the mind to seek mind, this is relying on the outside to learn (and copy) something from it; what then will you achieve?

13. Śramaṇa: ascetic of all kinds, or a Buddhist monk who has left his family and passions behind. Śramaṇa also means very difficult achievement, diligent stilling of the mind and the passions, purity of mind, and poverty. A Śramaṇa must uphold the Truth, guard well every uprising of desire, be uncontaminated by external attractions, be merciful to all and impure to none, not be elated by joy nor harrowed by distress and be able to bear whatever may come.

Śramaṇa should not be confounded with śrāmaṇera, a male novice and śrāmaṇerikā, a female novice.

The ancients had sharp minds and as soon as they heard of a (teaching) word, they immediately stopped learning; hence they were called 'Men of Tao in their non-active and beyond learning states'.[14] Nowadays, people want to widen their knowledge and interpretation by gathering meanings in the scriptures, and call this their practice without appreciating that wide knowledge and interpretation can turn into obstruction (to their realization of the Truth). This is like giving too much butter to a baby without knowing if it can digest it or not. Students of the Three Vehicles (of śrāvakas, pratyeka-buddhas and Bodhisattvas) are all like this and are called those who do not digest what they eat.

Therefore, all knowledge and interpretation which are not assimilable, are poisons, for they drive people into the realm of birth and death. There is no such thing in the absolute state of suchness (Bhūtatathatā). Hence it is said that "in my royal storehouse there is no such sword."

You should banish from and empty yourself of all previous (knowledge and) interpretation; this is the void Tathāgata Store. If the Tathāgata Store is empty of even the finest dust (that was there before) this is wiping out what *is* and means the Dharma-rāja (the King of the Law or the Buddha) appearing in the world, which also means "When the Tathāgata was with Dīpaṁkara, He did not obtain anything from the Dharma".[15]

This (last) sentence serves to empty yourself of all passionate interpretation and knowing capacity, and by exhausting all feelings within and without so that nothing remains, you will become an unconcerned man.

The teaching of the Three Vehicles are only medicines

14. Quote from Yung Chia's Song of Enlightenment (first two verses). Cf *Ch'an and Zen Teaching, Third Series*, page 116 (Rider, London; Shambala, Berkeley).

15. Quote from the Diamond Sūtra. Cf *Ch'an and Zen Teaching, Series One*, page 172, last paragraph. (Rider, London; Shambala, Berkeley).

prescribed to responsive potentialities. All preachings according to circumstances and all temporary methods of teaching differ from one another. If you are clear about them, you are not deceived by them. The most important thing is not to cling to individual capability and special teaching words, in order to interpret the scriptures. Why so? Because "there is no fixed Dharma the Tathāgata can expound".[16]

This sect of mine does not discuss all this. It will suffice to know how to rest the mind (and nothing else), for there is no need to think of yesterday and to worry about the morrow.'

The monk asked, 'It is always said that mind is Buddha but I do not know which mind is Buddha.'

The master asked back, 'How many minds do you have?'

The monk asked, 'Is the wordly mind or the holy mind Buddha?'

The master asked back, 'Where are your worldly and holy minds?'

The monk said, 'The Three Vehicles speak of the worldly and holy minds; how can you say they are not?'

The master said, 'The Three Vehicles clearly say that both the worldly and holy minds are false. You do not understand the teaching and now regard both as existing. You take what is false for the real, is this not wrong? Because you are wrong, your mind is deluded. But just banish both the worldly and holy states and there will be no other Buddha outside your mind.

The Patriarch came from the West to give a direct indication that all men are wholly Buddhas. Now because you do not know this, you grasp the worldly and the holy and let your mind wander outside thereby deluding itself. Hence you are told that mind is identical with Buddha. As soon as

16. Quote from the Diamond Sūtra. Cf *Ch'an and Zen Teaching, First Series*, page 168, 4th paragraph. (Rider, London; Shambala, Berkeley).

a worldly thought arises, you immediately slip into heterodoxy.

Since time without beginning, the mind has never differed
from what it is today. Because there is no different Dharma,
it is called supreme enlightenment (samyaksambodhi).'

The monk asked, 'What is the reason for your use of (the
word) identical?'

The master replied, 'What reason do you search for? As
soon as there is some reason, your mind will differ (from
what it fundamentally is).'

The monk asked, 'You have said that since time without
beginning it has never differed from what it is today; what
does this mean?'

The master replied, 'It is because of your search for it that
you differ from it. If you do not search, what is the difference?'

The monk asked, 'If it has never differed, why did you
say that it is identical?'

The master replied, 'If you do not hold on to the worldly
and the holy (states) who will tell you about the identical? If
the identical is no longer identical, the mind also will no
longer be mind, thereby banishing both the identical and the
mind, then where will you make your search?'

The monk asked, 'As falsehood screens the self-mind, what
should be used to wipe out falsehood?'

The master replied, 'The false (idea) of wiping out falsehood is also a falsehood. Falsehood is rootless and springs
from discrimination. Now if you only cease discriminating
between the worldly and the holy, falsehood will be no more.
How then can you wipe it out? You should refrain from even
the least clinging to it, and this is the meaning of the sentence,
"I give up my two arms[17] and am bound to be a Buddha."

The monk asked, 'If there is no clinging, what then is to
be transmitted (from master to pupil)?'

17. Two arms here stand for the dual conception of things.

The master replied, 'The mind is used in this transmission (of mind).'

The monk asked, 'If the mind is used in the transmission of mind, then why did you say that there is no mind?'

The master replied, 'The non-acquisition of a single thing is called the transmission of mind. If you are clear about this mind, there is no mind and also no Dharma.'

The monk asked, 'If there be neither mind nor Dharma (thing) what does the transmission stand for?'

The master replied, 'When you hear about the transmission of mind, you wrongly think that there is something to be gained. Hence the Patriarch said:

> Only when the nature of the mind is realized
> Can one say that it cannot be conceived.
> Nothing, clearly, can be realized
> For if it be, there's no awareness of it.'[18]

'How can this be taught fittingly to awaken worldly men?'

The monk asked, 'Is the space in front of us an object? Is it possible to perceive the mind without being shown its object?'

The master said, 'Which mind teaches you to perceive itself by means of its object? Even if you could perceive it, it would be a (subjective) mind which sees its object. This is like a man looking at his face in a mirror. Although he sees clearly his eyebrows and eyes, they are just an image. What connection does this image have with your mind?'

The monk asked, 'If its reflection does not come into play, when can the mind be perceived?'

The master said, 'If this implies a cause, which means that you must always rely on objects, when will you be awakened (to the absolute mind)? Have you not read these lines:

18. The gāthā of transmission chanted by the 23rd Indian Patriarch Haklena. Cf *Ch'an and Zen Teaching, Second Series*, page 46. (Rider, London; Shambala, Berkeley).

"Suddenly it resembles you but there is not a (real) thing,
It is sterile to discuss it in several thousand ways."'

The monk asked, 'When it is thoroughly known, is it true
that there is nothing (that can be) reflected?'

The master replied, 'If there is nothing, what is the use of
reflecting? Do not open your eyes while talking in your
sleep.'

*

(One day) the master ascended to the Ch'an hall and said
to the assembly, 'Hundreds of kinds of knowledge cannot
compare to the absence of desire which is unsurpassable. The
man of Tao is one who is unconcerned in everything. In
reality there are not so many sorts of minds and there is not
even that unconcerned (state). The meeting is now dismissed.'

*

(One day) a monk asked the master, 'What is worldly
truth?'[19]

The master replied, 'What is the use of talking about
creepers?[20] That which is fundamentally pure and clean, is
beyond word, speech, question and answer. The absence of
all sorts of (different) minds is called transcendental wisdom.

In your daily activities, whether walking, standing, sitting
or reclining, your words and speeches should be disengaged
from the worldly way of life thereby (causing) all your
utterances to become transcendental (non-dual) in the
twinkling of an eye. At present, in this Dharma ending age,
most students of Ch'an cling to all sorts of sounds and forms.
Why do not they, together with me, reduce the mind to the
state of empty space, of a withered log, of a stone, of cold
ashes and extinct fire? Only then can there be some little

19. As contrasted with the truth in reality as taught by the Buddha.
20. Creepers: clinging vines that hide the trunk of a large tree or the
real thing that counts.

degree of responsiveness (to the absolute thatness), otherwise they will have later to be flogged by Yama (the god of the hell for their sins).

You will have only to keep from all that *is* and *is not* so that your mind will be solitary like the sun in midheaven, bright and shining by itself. Does not this save a great deal of vigour? When you reach this stage, there will be no fixed abode to stay at as you tread the Buddha path, which means 'developing a mind which does not abide in anything'.[21] This is your pure and clean Dharmakāya which is called Anubodhi (Supreme Enlightenment). If you do not awaken to it, although you may gather wide knowledge and have done austerities by wearing clothing made of grass and by eating wild plants, your non-cognizance of the mind is called heresy and you will join the retinue of heavenly demons. What advantage do you gain from such practice? Hence Ch'an master Pao Chih said, 'Buddha being basically the self-mind, how can it be found in books?'

Even if you succeed in learning the three virtuous stages,[22] the four grades of Hīnayāna saintship,[23] and the ten highest stages of Bodhisattva attainments[24] your whole mind still remains within the worldly and holy realms. Have you not read this sentence: 'All phenomenal changes belong to the

21. Quote from the Diamond Sūtra. Cf *Ch'an and Zen Teaching, First Series*, page 173, paragraph 5 (Rider, London; Shambala, Berkeley)

22. The three virtuous stages: (a) the ten practical stages of Bodhisattva-wisdom; (b) the ten lines of Bodhisattva action; and (c) the ten acts of dedication. Cf *The Śūraṅgama Sūtra* pages 167-170 (Rider, London).

23. The four grades of Hīnayāna saintship: śrota-āpanna-phala, one who has entered the stream of holy living; sakṛ-dāgāmi-phala, once more to come, or be born; anāgāmi-phala, a non-coming or non-returning arhat who will not be reborn; and arhat, a saintly man, the highest type or ideal saint in Hīnayāna in contrast with a Bodhisattva as the saint in Mahāyāna.

24. The ten highest stages of Bodhisattva attainment (Daśabhūmi). Cf *The Śūraṅgama Sūtra*, page 172. (Rider, London).

realm of birth and death' and also (the following verses:)

> With force expended, a spent arrow is bound to fall and cause
> Distasteful things to follow in the next incarnation.
> How can it then compare with the wu wei reality,
> Which ensures a leap straight to the Tathāgata stage?[25]

Since you are not a man of such calibre you should follow the converting instruction devised by the ancients in order to widen your knowledge and interpretation.

Ch'an master Pao Chih said, 'If you do not meet with an enlightened master appearing in the world, you will vainly take the Dharma-medicine of Mahāyāna.'

Now if you only learn to develop unmindfulness at all times while walking, standing, sitting and reclining, you may fail, in the course of time, to leap over (to Reality) solely because of your insufficient strength; but if you so continue for another three, five or ten years until you enter (reality), you will surely awaken to it (in the end). It is because you cannot do so that you set your mind on the study of Ch'an and Tao, which is irrelevant to the Buddha-Dharma.

Hence the sūtra says, 'I have not gained even the least (bit of) Dharma, and this is called supreme enlightenment.[26] If you understand this, you will realize that the realm of Buddha and that of demons are both false and that the real is fundamentally pure, clean, immaculate, neither square nor round, neither great nor small, neither long nor short; it is transcendental and non-active (wu wei) and neither deluded nor enlightened (because)

> To him who sees clearly that there is not a thing,
> There is not a man and also not a Buddha.

25. Quote from Yung Chia's Song of Enlightenment. Cf *Ch'an and Zen Teaching, Third Series*, page 127. (Rider, London; Shambala, Berkeley).
26. Quote from the Diamond Sūtra. Cf *Ch'an and Zen Teaching, First Series,* page 197, third paragraph. (Rider, London; Shambala, Berkeley).

Countless worlds in the great chiliocosm are only bubbles
In the sea (while) all saints and sages are but lightning
flashes.[27]

For nothing can compare with a mind set on Reality. From
time immemorial until now (your) Dharmakāya has not
differed from those of the Buddhas and Patriarchs; where
then is a deficiency of the size of a minute hair? If you understand this, you should strive (to realize it) during your present
lifetime because (impermanence is quick to come and) an out
breath does not guarantee the following in breath.'

The monk asked, 'Why did the Sixth Patriarch who (was
illiterate and) did not even know the sūtras, inherit the
patriarchate whereas Shen Hsiu did not, although he taught
the 500 monks of the community of which he was the head
and had expounded thirty-two sūtras and śāstras?'

The master replied, 'Because he (Shen Hsiu) kept a worldly
mind and his practice and realization were also on an earthly
plane. Hence the Fifth Patriarch transmitted the robe to the
Sixth Patriarch who intuitively agreed with the Buddha's
profound revelation which was esoterically handed down to
him; this is why he inherited the Dharma. Have you not
read the following gāthā (of transmission):

> The Dharma's fundamental Dharma has no Dharma,
> The Dharma of No-Dharma is Dharma too.
> Now that the Dharma of No-Dharma is transmitted,
> Has there ever been a Dharma?[28]

Only when you understand this gāthā can you be called
a home leaver and practise (the Dharma). If you do not
believe me, ask yourself why when Hui Ming in pursuit of
the Sixth Patriarch arrived at Ta Yu Ling (mountain range),

27. Quote from Yung Chia's Song of Enlightenment. Cf *Ch'an and
Zen Teaching, Third Series* page 144 (Rider, London; Shambala, Berkeley).
28. Śākyamuni Buddha's transmission gāthā. Cf *Ch'an and Zen Teaching,
Second Series* page 31 (Rider, London; Shambala, Berkeley).

the latter asked him, 'What do you want, the robe or the Dharma?' Hui Ming replied, 'I do not come for the robe but for the Dharma.' The Patriarch said, 'Think of neither good nor evil (to stop the thinking process); at this very moment (when no thoughts arise in your mind) what is the Venerable Hui Ming's fundamental face before he was born?'

Hearing these words Hui Ming suddenly awakened intuitively (to Reality) and paid his obeisance to the Patriarch, saying, 'It is like drinking water which the drinker alone knows whether it is cold or warm. I have stayed with the Fifth Patriarch for thirty years and only today do I realize that I have wasted all my time to no purpose.' The Patriarch said, 'It is so.'[29]

It is at that very moment (of awakening) that one knows that the real purpose of the Patriarch coming from the West was to point direct at the mind for the perception of self-nature and attainment of Buddhahood. All this does not lie in words and speech.

Have you not read that when Ānanda asked Mahākāśyapa, 'What Dharma did the World Honoured One especially hand down beside the kāṣāya robe?',[30] Mahākāśyapa called, 'Ānanda'. Ānanda answered, 'Present!' Mahākāśyapa then ordered him, 'Pull down the flagpole in front of the monastery.'[31] This is the Patriarch's pattern of mind transmission.[32]

Ānanda who was the Buddha's attendant for thirty years during which he acquired a very wide knowledge of the

29. A term of approval of the pupil's awakening.

30. Kāṣāya: a robe embroidered with gold.

31. Ānanda's word 'Present!' reveals the mind which directs him to answer Mahākāśyapa's call. Mahākāśyapa's order to pull down the flagpole reveals the functioning of Ānanda's mind. Hence Ānanda realizes both the substance and function of his Buddha-nature which manifest when the mind is pure and clean.

32. This is Ānanda's great awakening which entitled him to be the second Indian Patriarch of the Transmission of Mind outside the Teaching. Cf Ch'an and Zen Teaching, Second Series, page 32 (Rider, London; Shambala, Berkeley).

Dharma, was (later) scolded by the World Honoured One who said, 'Your one thousand days devoted to the study of prajñā cannot compare to a day of practice of Tao. If you do not train in Tao you will be unable to digest a drop of water.'

A home leaver should be clear about the aim (of the Transmission of Mind) which has been handed down from time out of mind. For instance, Niu T'ou who was a disciple of the Fourth Patriarch and could preach (the Dharma) in many different ways, did not yet know the upper keystone the Eye of which alone enables one to distinguish between heterodoxy and orthodoxy and the unauthentic and the authentic. And those who cannot awaken (to the absolute) learn only words and speech, turn their attention to the skin bag (the human body) and then proclaim everywhere they go that they know Ch'an. Can they really help you escape from birth and death? These careless old masters will fall into hell with the speed of a (flying) arrow.

'As soon as I see them enter the door I immediately know them. Do you understand this? Waste no time and strive to realize the truth. Do not treat this question lightly. Do not spend your life aimlessly and do not allow yourself to be a laughing stock for those who see clearly. Later you will not escape from being deceived by worldlings. You should ponder over all this carefully and see to whom it is a matter of concern. If you understand it, you will grasp it here and now but if you do not, go away and take care of yourself.'

*

When a monk asked the master, 'What is the aim of the coming from the West?' the master gave him a stroke of the staff.

From then on his teaching was for disciples of high potentiality. As to those of medium and low spirituality, they were unable to fathom his Dharma.

During the Ta Chung reign (847–860) of the T'ang dynasty, the master passed away on Huang Po mountain. The emperor conferred upon him the posthumous title of Ch'an master Tuan Chi (Cutter of Time) and upon his stūpa the epitaph of Kuang Yeh (Extensive Deeds).

*

From the Wan Ling record

Chancellor Pei Hsiu asked the master, 'There is on the mountain a community of four to five hundred persons; how many of them have realized the Dharma as expounded by the Venerable Master?'

Huang Po replied, 'The number of those realizing the Dharma is unaccountable. Why is it so? Because Tao is realized by the mind and not (by means of) words and speech, for words and speech serve only to convert beginners'.

Pei Hsiu asked, 'What is Buddha?'

Huang Po replied, 'Mind is Buddha and unmindfulness is Tao (the path). Just refrain from stirring the thinking process and from setting the mind on what *is* and *is not*, long and short, the self and others, and subject and object. Mind is fundamentally Buddha, and Buddha is basically mind. Mind is like empty space; hence it is said that the Buddha's true Dharmakāya is like empty space. There is no need to seek it elsewhere, for all longing results in suffering. Even if you pass aeons as countless as the sand grains in the Ganges to practise the six perfections (pāramitā) and a myriad lines of Bodhisattva conduct in order to realize the Buddha-bodhi, it will not be the ultimate one. Why? Because it is causally produced and when its cause comes to an end, it will return to the condition of impermanence.

Hence it is said, 'The Sambhogakāya and Nirmāṇakāya are not real Buddhas and are not the preachers of the Dharma.' Just recognize the self-mind, free from selfness and otherness, as fundamentally Buddha.'

Pei Hsiu asked, 'A saintly man who is unmindful is a Buddha, but does a worldly man who is unmindful sink into emptiness?'

Huang Po replied, 'The Dharma is neither worldly nor saintly; it also does not sink into emptiness. Fundamentally the Dharma *is not* but do not hold the view of its non-existence. The Dharma is fundamentally not non-existing but do not hold the view of its existence. For *is* and *is not* are wrong views created by passion, like things seen by a bad eye. Hence it is said:

"Seeing and hearing are like optical illusions;
While the illusory knower becomes a living being."[33]

Our Patriarchs' sect formulates only the resting of potentiality and the end of all views. Hence the resting of potentiality causes the Buddha-truth to prosper whereas discrimination causes the army of māras (demons) to flourish.'

Pei Hsiu asked, 'If the mind is fundamentally Buddha is it still necessary to practise the six perfections (pāramitā) and the myriad lines of Bodhisattva conduct?'

The master replied, 'Awakening comes from the mind and does not concern the six pāramitās and myriad lines of Bodhisattva conduct. For the six pāramitās and myriad lines of Bodhisattva conduct are concerned with the conversion and guidance of living beings for their salvation.

Even bodhi, the absolute (suchness), reality, liberation, Dharmakāya, the ten highest stages of Bodhisattva attainment and the four states of Hīnayāna sainthood, are all doors to liberation but are irrelevant to Buddha and mind, for mind is but Buddha. Hence of all doors to liberation, Buddha and mind are the highest. If we only refrain from setting the mind on birth and death, kleśa (troubles), etc., there will be

33. Quote from Mañjuśri's gāthā. Cf *The Śūrangama Sūtra* page 143 verse 8 and page 148 verse 15.

no need for bodhi, etc. Hence it is said, 'The Buddha preaches all sorts of Dharmas to deliver all sorts of discriminating minds, but (if) I am free from such minds, what then is the use of these Dharmas?' From Buddhas to Patriarchs nothing was discussed beyond the one-mind which is also called the one-vehicle. Hence there are no other vehicles for all seekers (of the Truth) in the ten directions. This vehicle is twigless and formulates only (one) reality. Hence it is not easy to believe this doctrine.

When Bodhidharma came to this country, in the two kingdoms of Liang and Wei that he visited he found only the great master Hui K'o who believed in the self-mind and awakened to it upon hearing the (Indian) patriarch's words. Cognizance of the self-mind as Buddha with the non-existence of body and mind, is the great Tao (great way) which is fundamentally universal. Hence the profound belief that all sentient beings are of one real (underlying) nature. When self-mind and self-nature do not differ from each other, the self-nature is but the mind. When the mind does not differ from the self-nature it is called the Patriarch. Hence it is said,

> Only when the nature of the mind is realized
> Can one say that it cannot be conceived.[34]

Pei Hsiu asked, 'Did the Buddha (actually) liberate living beings?'

The master replied, 'There were really no living beings whom the Tathāgata could liberate.[35] If even myself (my ego) cannot be found (to exist) how can those who are not myself (my ego) be found (to exist)? For both Buddha and living beings cannot be found (anywhere).'

34. The first two verses of the 23rd Indian Patriarch Haklena's transmission gāthā. Cf *Ch'an and Zen Teaching, Second Series*, page 46 (Rider, London; Shambala, Berkeley).

35. Quote from the Diamond Sūtra. Cf *Ch'an and Zen Teaching, First Series*, page 198, paragraph 4 (Rider, London; Shambala, Berkeley).

Pei Hsiu asked, 'The Buddha appeared in the world with thirty-two physical marks to liberate living beings; how can he be said to be non-existent?'

The master replied, 'Everything with form is unreal; if all forms are seen as unreal, the Tathāgata will be perceived.[36]

For Buddha and living beings are all created by your perverse views. It is because you do not know your fundamental mind that you hold the view of Buddha which hinders you. As soon as you hold the view of living beings, you are hindered by it. The views of the worldly, of the saintly, of purity and impurity, if you hold on to them, all hinder your mind which will subject you to transmigratory existences. This is like the monkeys one has caught; if one monkey is released and another is caught, there will be no end to this series of freeing and catching.

It is most important for the student to stop all studies and to keep from both the worldly and the saintly, purity and impurity, big and small (things) as well as from all mundane activities in order to achieve the one-mind which should be expediently embellished by moral actions.

Even if you succeeded in studying the three vehicles and the twelve divisions of the (Mahāyāna) canon, you should relinquish all views and interpretations; hence the emptying of the house (of all attendants and furniture except) a sick bed for Vimalakīrti to lay on.[37] This means the non-rising of all sorts of views and the non-acquisition of anything whatever in order to be released from Dharma-hindrance and to leap over and beyond all worldly and saintly states in the three worlds (of desire, form and beyond form). Only then can one become a Buddha appearing in the world. Hence

36. Quote from the Diamond Sūtra. Cf *Ch'an and Zen Teaching, First Series*, page 165, paragraph 7 (Rider, London; Shambala, Berkeley).

37. Quote from the *Vimalakīrti Nirdeśa Sūtra*, Chapter 5, Mañjuśri's call on Vimalakīrti page 49, paragraph 4 (Shambala, Berkeley; Routledge & Kegan Paul Ltd, London).

'I bow to Him who, like space, relies on nothing!'[38] – thereby leaping over heresies.

When the mind does not differentiate, the Dharma also is free from discrimination. When the mind is inactive (wu wei) the Dharma is also non-creative. For all things are just transformations of the mind. So when 'my' mind is void, all dharmas (things) are also void, with the result that thousands and tens of thousands, of various things come to an end. Space in the ten directions being pervaded by the substance of the one-mind, when the latter does not differentiate, all things (in space) are non-discriminative.

It is only your views and interpretations which differ from each other. This is like the gods using the same precious vessels when they take their meals, but the colour of the rice they eat differs according to the degree of their meritorious achievements.

The Buddhas in the ten directions did not really win the least bit of Dharma, and this is called Anubodhi[39] which is not variegated forms and is just the one-mind that is neither bright nor dull and neither wins nor loses (anything). It does not win and so is not in the form of a Buddha, and it does not lose so is not in the form of a living being.'

Pei Hsiu asked, 'If the mind is formless, do you mean that the Buddha does not have the thirty-two physical marks and eighty accompanying excellent characteristics when he appears to convert and deliver living beings?'

The master replied. 'The thirty-two physical marks pertain to form, and all forms are unreal.[39] The eighty accompanying excellent characteristics belong to the material (body) and he who seeks to perceive the Buddha by means of his body

38. Quote from *The Vimalakīrti Nirdeśa Sūtra*, Chapter One, The Buddha-land, page 8, the last verse of Ratna-rāśi's gāthā of praise to the Buddha (Shambala, Berkeley; Routledge and Kegan Paul Ltd., London)

39. Quote from The Diamond Sūtra. Cf *Ch'an and Zen Teaching, First series*, part III (Rider, London; Shambala, Berkeley).

143

treads the heterodox path and is unable to perceive the Tathātaga.[39]

Pei Hsiu asked, 'Is the Buddha-nature identical with or different from the nature of a living being?'

The master replied, 'Their natures are neither identical nor different. According to the Teachings of the Three Vehicles (of śrāvakas, pratyeka-buddhas and Bodhisattvas), there are the Buddha-nature and the nature of a living being. Therefore, the law of causality as taught by the Three Vehicles, specifies both identical and different natures. But the Buddha-vehicle and the Transmission handed down from past patriarchs, do not discuss this; they only point to the One-mind which is neither identical nor different, and is neither cause nor effect. Hence it is said that there is only one vehicle with neither a second nor a third one[40] unless the Buddha preaches in an expedient (upāya) way.'

Pei Hsiu asked, 'Why did the Boundless Bodied Bodhisattva fail to perceive the crown of the Buddha?'

The master replied, 'Really it cannot be seen. Why? Because the Boundless Bodied Bodhisattva is just the Tathāgata who should not be seen further.[41] This is only to teach you not to hold on to the view of Buddha in order not to fall into the (objective) Buddha realm; not to hold on to the view of living beings in order not to fall into the (objective) realm of living beings; not to hold on to the concept of *is* in order not to fall into (objective) existence; not to hold on to the concept of *is not* in order not to fall into (objective) non-existence; not to hold on to the worldly view in order not to fall into the (objective) worldly realm; and not to hold on to the holy view in order not to fall into the (objective) holy realm, for he who keeps from all views is the Boundless Bodied Bodhisattva. He who is immersed in views is a heretic, for heresy delights in all sorts of views. As to the

40. Quote from the Lotus Sūtra.
41. In order to keep from the duality of subjective seer and the objective seen.

144

Bodhisattva, he remains immutable when confronting all views. For 'Tathāgata' means the suchness of all dharmas (things).[42] Hence it is said, 'Maitreya is also in this suchness, and all saints and sages are equally in this suchness.'[43] This state of suchness is beyond birth and death and is above seeing and hearing. The crown of the Tathāgata is neither a perfect nor an imperfect view and, therefore, does not fall on the side of perfection.[44] Hence the Buddha-body is wu wei (non-creative) and does not fall into fate and destiny.

It is expediently compared to space and referred to as integral as the great emptiness which is neither deficient nor excessive, and is truly carefree and at ease. All arbitrary speculation about its state belongs to consciousness. Hence it is said, 'The (concept of its) perfection results in a slip into the sea of consciousness and will cause you to drift about like straws floating (in water). Then you will be led to proclaim, 'I know it', 'I have succeeded in practising it', 'I am awakened to it', 'I am liberated' and 'This is the noumenon'. When you are approved by others you are joyful but when you are criticized you are angry. Thus you seem to interpret correctly but what is the usefulness of all this?

I now tell you, 'Be carefree and at ease' and do not deceive yourself by the wrong use of your mind. 'Do not seek the real, but your false views lay down'.[45] Therefore, all views, both inner and outer, are wrong. The Buddha-path and the demon-path are both evil. Hence for giving rise to a dual view Mañjuśrī was banished to the two iron mountain ranges

42. Quote from the Diamond Sūtra. Cf *Ch'an and Zen Teaching, First Series*, page 190 last paragraph. (Rider, London; Shambala, Berkeley).

43. Quote from *The Vimalakīrti Nirdeśa Sūtra*, Chapter 4, page 37. Maitreya meeting Vimalakīrti. (Shambala, Berkeley; Routledge & Kegan Paul Ltd, London).

44. Perfection and imperfection are the two extremes of a duality which is illusory.

45. Quote from the Third Patriarch's gāthā 'Have faith in your Mind'. Cf *Practical Buddhism*. (Rider, London; Theosophical Publishing House, Wheaton, USA).

that encircles the world. Mañjuśrī symbolizes the absolute wisdom and Samantabhadra symbolizes the expedient (upāya) wisdom. Both absolute and relative wisdoms are opposites to and are used to set off each other, but in reality there is neither absolute nor expedient wisdom. For there is only the One-mind which is neither Buddha (enlightened) nor living being (unenlightened) and is free from differentiated views. As soon as a view of Buddha arises, it is immediately followed by that of a living being. The rising views of *is*, of *is not*, of permanence and of impermanence become the two iron mountain ranges (that obstruct wisdom).

Hence the Patriarch points direct to the very substance of the mind of all living beings which is fundamentally Buddha, and which cannot be realized by practice and which does not come about gradually step by step, for it is neither light nor darkness. Because it is not light it is beyond enlightenment, and because it is not darkness it is above unenlightenment. Hence it is beyond both ignorance and the end of ignorance.[46]

On being initiated into this sect of mine you should ponder over all this. Your skill to see (things) in this way is called Dharma, and he who sees into the Dharma is called Buddha. He who no longer holds on to both Buddha and Dharma is (a member of the) Saṅgha, also called a non-creative (wu wei) order or the Three Gems in One Body. For a seeker of the Dharma does not hold on to Buddha, Dharma and Saṅgha. He should seek nothing, for non-seeking of Buddha is the non-existence of (the objective) Buddha; non-seeking of Dharma is the non-existence of (the objective) Dharma; and non-seeking of the Order is the non-existence of (the objective) Saṅgha.

Pei Hsiu asked the master, 'The Venerable Sir sees people preach the Dharma; then how can he say there is neither Saṅgha nor Dharma?'

46. Quote from the Heart Sūtra. Cf *Ch'an and Zen Teaching, First Series*, page 216, paragraph 5 (Rider, London; Shambala, Berkeley).

The master replied, 'If you think there is a Dharma that can be preached, this is (what the Diamond Sūtra) calls "Seeing me in sound".[47] If you see me, this implies a place (which is wrong). Dharma also is not really Dharma, for Dharma is but the mind. Hence it is said:

> As this Mind-Dharma is now transmitted
> Which Dharma is the real one?
> Only when Dharma and self-mind vanish
> Can Mind-Dharma be understood.

For in reality there is not a single Dharma that can be realized; this is called sitting in a bodhimaṇḍala (a holy site). By a holy site is meant the non-rising of views. Awakening to the Dharma which is fundamentally immaterial is called the noumenal Tathāgata store (k'ung ju lai tsang).

If you gather the true meaning of the following two lines of verse you will rise above and beyond all discussion:

> In essence there is not a thing;
> On what then can dust gather?[48]

Pei Hsiu asked, 'Is not the absence of objects precisely that state where, in essence, there is not a thing?'

The master replied, 'Absence is also not correct, for bodhi is beyond location and above knowledge and understanding.'

Pei Hsiu asked, 'Then what is Buddha?'

The master replied, 'Your mind is Buddha and Buddha is but mind. Mind and Buddha do not differ from one another, hence it is said that mind is identical with Buddha. For apart from the mind there is no Buddha.'

Pei Hsiu asked, 'If the mind is Buddha, how could the

---

47. Quote from the Diamond Sūtra. Cf *Ch'an and Zen Teaching, First Series*, page 199, The Buddha's gāthā. (Rider, London; Shambala, Berkeley).

48. Quote from the Sixth Patriarch's gāthā. Cf *Ch'an and Zen Teaching, Third Series*, page 24. (Rider, London; Shambala, Berkeley).

Patriarch who came from the West hand down the Transmission?'

The master replied, 'The Patriarch coming from the West transmitted only the Mind-Buddha, and pointed directly to your mind which is essentially Buddha. He whose mind does not differentiate is a Patriarch. If you understand (experience) this you will leap over the Three Vehicles (of śrāvakas, pratyeka-buddhas and Bodhisattvas) and all stages of Bodhisattva development (into Buddhahood). For you are fundamentally Buddha, and this cannot be attained by practice.'

Pei Hsiu asked, 'If this is so what Dharma did the Buddhas preach when they appeared in the world?'

The master replied, 'The Buddha in the ten directions appeared in the world to proclaim only one Mind-Dharma which Śākyamuni Buddha handed down to Mahākāśyapa. The substance of this one Mind-Dharma pervades all immaterial and material worlds and is the doctrine proclaimed by all Buddhas. How then can you understand it by means of words and letters in your discussions? Moreover it cannot be realized by means of a single potential or a single field of mind. For it can only be experienced intuitively. This is the non-creative (wu wei) Dharma-door (to enlightenment). If you really want to realize it you should know that unmindfulness can result in sudden awakening to it. If you use your (discriminating) mind to study it you will keep yourself far away from it. If your mind is free from crookedness and from accepting or rejecting, and if it is as insensible as a piece of wood or a stone there will be some chance for you to study the Tao.'

Pei Hsiu asked, 'Are we not full of wrong thoughts now? How can you speak of thoughtlessness?'

The master replied, 'Falsehood has no substance of its own and arises from your mind. If you recognize that mind is Buddha and is free from falsehood, how can falsehood arise in the mind to be clung to? If you do not stir the mind and do not give rise to thoughts, naturally there will be no false-hood. Hence it is said, "When the mind arises, it creates all things; and when the mind stops arising all things come to an end".'

Pei Hsiu asked, 'When false thoughts arise where is the Buddha?'

The master replied, 'Now as you are aware of the rise of false thoughts, the awareness of that which is not false is awareness of the Buddha. When your false thoughts come to an end even the idea of Buddha is no more. Why so? Because when you stir your mind with the idea of Buddha you think of Buddhahood which can be attained. If you hold the view of living beings you will think of living beings who can be liberated. Therefore, the stirring mind and rising thoughts are the causes of your differentiated views.

If you are free from all sorts of views, where can the Buddha be located? Therefore, when Mañjuśrī gave rise to the view of Buddha he was banished to the second range of iron mountains that encircle the world.'

Pei Hsiu asked, 'At the time of enlightenment where is the Buddha?'

The master replied, 'Where does your question come from and where does your awareness arise? For speech, silence, motion and stillness as well as all sounds and forms proclaim the Buddha-truth. Where else do you want to seek Buddha? Do not put another head on your own head, and do not place another mouth on your own mouth. Just do not give rise to differentiated views, for mountains are mountains, rivers are rivers, saṅgha is saṅgha, and the laity are laity, because mountains, rivers, the great earth, the sun, the moon, stars and planets are not outside your mind. The great chiliocosm (tri-sahasra-mahā-sahasra-loka-dhātu) arises from your own self. Where then are so many things? Because outside the mind there is not a thing. Before your eyes are blue moun-tains, empty space and the world at large, but clearly there is not a thing as tiny as a speck that is an object of your (distorted) views. Hence it is said that all sounds and forms (reveal) the Buddha-wisdom. For no dharma (thing) can arise of itself but depends on an (objective) field to manifest, thereby giving rise to a number of wisdoms based on the number of (appearing) phenomena. So the Dharma is preached the whole day long but what Dharma is actually spoken? The Dharma is heard the whole day long but what Dharma is actually heard? Hence Śākyamuni Buddha preached the Dharma for forty-nine years without actually speaking a single word.'

Pei Hsiu asked, 'If so where is Bodhi?'

The master replied, 'Bodhi is nowhere. The Buddha does not win Bodhi and living beings do not lose it, for Bodhi cannot be realized by the body and cannot be sought by the mind. All living beings are the expression of Bodhi.'

Pei Hsiu asked, 'How then can one develop the Bodhi-mind?'

The master replied, 'Bodhi means the non-winning of anything. If you now set your mind on gainlessness with decisively not a thing to be won, this is Bodhi-mind. For Bodhi has no abode which explains its gainlessness. Hence "when I was with Dīpaṁkara Buddha, I did not gain anything from the Dharma. This is why he predicted my future attainment of Buddhahood."[49] It is quite clear that fundamentally all living beings possess Bodhi; they should not acquire it once more. Now that you hear about developing a Bodhi-mind you think of using a mind to study aspiring to be a Buddha in order to tread the Buddha-path. Even if you pass three asaṅkhya (endless aeons) for your practice and training you will achieve only the states of Sambhogakāya (reward body) and Nirmāṇakāya (transformation body) which have nothing in common with your fundamental self-

49. Quote from the Diamond Sūtra. Cf *Ch'an and Zen Teaching, First Series*, page 190 (Rider, London; Shambala, Berkeley).

natured Buddha. Hence it is said that to seek an external Buddha having a form does not give rise to one even resembling yours.'

Pei Hsiu asked, 'If man is fundamentally Buddha, how can there be four types of rebirth, six different realms of existence and different forms and shapes?'

The master replied, 'The substance of all Buddhas is perfect and neither increases nor decreases (in any circumstance). It remains perfect when entering upon the six worlds of existence; so everyone of the myriads of species is Buddha (in essence). This is like quicksilver poured on the ground which scatters in drops that are all round in shape. Before being poured it was a lump which illustrates (the state of) one in all and all in one. The various forms and appearances are like dwelling places to change which is like leaving a stable for donkeys to enter a house for man, or leaving a human body to enter the body of a deva or that of a śrāvaka, a pratyeka-buddha, a Bodhisattva or a Buddha. These different houses result from the accepting and rejecting mind and consequently differ from one another; but the fundamental nature is changeless.'

Pei Hsiu asked, 'What is vīrya (unfailing progress)?'

The master replied, 'The unstirred body and mind are the most vigorous vīrya. As soon as the mind is set on outer quest, this is Kalirāja who is fond of hunting, and if the mind is not set on externals this is Kṣāntyṛṣi.[50] When both body and mind are no more, this is the Buddha-path.'

Pei Hsiu asked, 'Does one win (Bodhi) if one is unmindful when treading this path?'

The master replied, 'Unmindfulness already means treading this path. Why do you still suggest winning and non-winning? The rise of a thought in your mind creates an object; if you

50. Quote from the Diamond Sūtra. Cf *Ch'an and Zen Teaching, First series*, page 182 last paragraph. (Rider, London; Shambala, Berkeley).

Kṣāntyṛṣi: a Ṛṣi who patiently suffered insult, i.e. Śākyamuni, in a former life, suffering mutilation to convert the hunter Kalirāja.

are unmindful this is the absence of the object while your mind will come to an end and cannot be searched for.'

Pei Hsiu asked, 'What should one do to get out of the three worlds (of desire, form and beyond form)?'

The master replied, 'Think of neither good nor evil and you will get out of the three worlds now at this very moment. The Tathāgata appeared in the world to cut off the (concept of) three worlds of existence. If one gets rid of all sorts of (differentiating) minds the three worlds do not really exist. This is like a speck of dust broken into a hundred parts; if ninety-nine parts are wiped out leaving behind one part which exists, the aim of Mahāyāna is not attained. If all the hundred parts are wiped out the Mahāyāna goal is achieved.'

*

The master once ascended to the meeting hall where he said to the assembly:

'Your very mind is Buddha. From all the Buddhas above to all sentient beings including wriggling worms below all possess the Buddha-nature and belong to the same substance of mind. Hence Bodhidharma came from the West to transmit only the One-mind Dharma according to which all living beings are fundamentally Buddhas and the state of Buddha is not attainable by practice. Now just (strive to) cognize your self-mind in order to perceive your self-nature (Chinese, chien hsing; Japanese, kensho) and do not seek anything else.

How do you cognize your self-mind? That which is speaking now is your mind. If you do not speak and also cease all activities, the substance of mind is like empty space without form and shape and without location and position; it has never been non-existent but is existing without being visible. Hence it is said, 'The mind-ground of true nature has neither head nor tail; its timely conversion of living beings is expediently called wisdom (prajñā). When it responds to ripening potentials it cannot be said to be existing or non-existent (but) at the time of its responsiveness it leaves no traces.

Now that you are aware of this, you should abide in nothingness, and this is called treading the path of all Buddhas. The sūtra says, 'You should develop a mind which does not abide in anything.'[51]

All living beings are subject to birth and death in their endless transmigrations because they use the sixth consciousness to move without pause through the six realms of existence thereby enduring all sorts of sufferings. Vimalakīrti said, 'Since the minds of those who are difficult to convert are like monkeys various methods of teaching are devised to check them so that they can be completely tamed.'[52] Hence it is said that when the mind stirs all things appear and when it ceases moving all things vanish. Therefore, we know that all things including the six worlds of men, devas, asuras, hells, etc. are all created by the mind.

Now you should learn only unmindfulness to wipe out all causality and refrain from giving rise to discriminatory thoughts in order to eliminate (all concepts of) selfness, otherness, desire, anger, like, dislike, gain, loss, etc. to recover the self-nature which is fundamentally pure and clean; this is the practice of Bodhi, Dharma and Buddhahood. If you do not understand this, although you may widen your knowledge, practise austerities, live on wild fruit and nuts and cover your body with grass and leaves, you will fail to realize your mind; this is just heterodoxy practised by heavenly demons and heretics,[53] and by ghosts and spirits in water and on land. What advantage can you expect from such practice.

51. Quote from the Diamond Sūtra. Cf *Ch'an and Zen Teaching, First Series*, page 173 paragraph 5 (Rider, London; Shambala, Berkeley).
52. Quote from *The Vimalakīrti Nirdeśa Sūtra*, Chapter 10 (Shambala, Berkeley; Routledge & Kegan Paul Ltd, London).
53. Both enemies of Buddha-truth.

Ch'an master Pao Chih said, 'Our fundamental substance is the self-mind; how can it be sought in books?' Now just cognize the self-mind and stop your thinking process, and kleśa (troubles) will come to an end. The Vimalakīti Nirdeśa Sūtra says, 'There was only a sick bed on which Vimalakīrti lay',[54] which means that the mind rests like a sick man on a bed whose clinging and perverse thoughts have come to an end; this is but Bodhi.

Now if your mind is unsettled, you may study the Three Vehicles, the four stages of Hīnayāna attainments and the ten degrees of Bodhisattva development into Buddhahood, but you will find yourself between the two extremes of the worldly and saintly states. And when your practice stops, its effects also come to an end like a flying arrow with force expended, which is bound to fall, and you will continue to transmigrate through the realms of birth and death. Is not such a practice, which fails to conform with the Buddha's teaching and causes aimless hardships and sufferings, a grave mistake?

Ch'an master Pao Chih said, 'He who has not met an enlightened master appearing in the world, wrongly takes the Mahāyāna medicine!'

Now at all times while you are walking, standing, sitting and reclining, practise only unmindfulness free from all differentiation, reliance and clinging, and pay no heed to anything, like a stupid man whom nobody wants to know and who does not want others to know him, with a dull mind like an insensible rock without fissures, which no externals can enter; if your mind is so intractable and does not cling to anything there will be some chance for you to fall in line (with absolute Reality) thereby leaping over the three worlds. Only then can you (aspire to be) a Buddha appearing in the

54. Cf *The Vimalakīrti Nirdeśa Sūtra*, Chapter 5. (Shambala, Berkeley; Routledge & Kegan Paul Ltd, London).

world (to liberate living beings). This passionless (anāsrava)[55] mind is called transcendental wisdom which will prevent you forming the (good) karma of men and devas and the (evil) karma of the hells, and will eliminate all causes that affect the mind. Your body and mind will be those of a kingly man; this does not mean that you are bodiless but that you can create a body at will (manomaya).[56] This is what the sūtra says about Bodhisattvas who can transform their bodies at will. If you are unable to realize unmindfulness and if you still cling to form, you will form the demonic karma. Even in your practice of the Pure Land (school) you will create a karma called the Buddha-screen which veils your mind thereby subjecting you to the law of causality; you will not be free to come and go (as all Bodhisattvas do). Hence all Dharmas including Bodhi do not actually exist but were expounded by the Tathāgata to convert worldlings like yellow leaves given to children as gold coins to keep them from crying. Therefore, there is really no Dharma called Anubodhi (Supreme Enlightenment).[57]

Now that you have understood all this, what is the use of roaming about (in your quest of the unreal)? Just adapt yourself to prevailing circumstances to requite your karmic debts but do not form fresh karma which will bring about new calamity. Thus the mind will be serene after all former views and interpretations have been thrown away. This is what Vimalakīrti meant by emptying his house of all his possessions.[58] The Lotus Sūtra says, 'For twenty years the son was

55. Anāsrava: passionless, outside the stream of transmigratory suffering; transcendental.

56. A Bodhisattva is able to take any form at will to liberate living beings.

57. Quote from The Diamond Sūtra. Cf Ch'an and Zen Teaching, First Series, part III, The Diamond Cutter of Doubts. (Rider, London; Shambala, Berkeley).

58. Quote from The Vimalakīrti Nirdeśa Sūtra, Chapter 5 (Shambala, Berkeley; Routledge & Kegan Paul Ltd, London).

ordered to remove excrement from the house' which means removing all views and interpretations from the mind. This sūtra also says, 'Remove the excrement of sophistry.'

So the Tathāgata store is fundamentally void and still and does not contain a single thing. Hence the sūtra says. 'The Buddha-lands are also void.'

He who claims that the Buddha-way can be attained by study and practice, makes an interpretation which is wholly irrelevant. When confronting some potentiality or situation he raises his eyebrows or winks in seeming response thereto and then claims that he awakens to and realizes the Ch'an Dharma. If someone fails to understand his claim he will accuse him of ignorance. If someone says that he wins Bodhi he is filled with joy. If someone criticizes his wrong claim he is filled with sorrow. If he so uses his intellect to practise Ch'an what relevancy does this bear? Even if you seem to realize something this something is an object of your (subjective) mind and has nothing in common with the Ch'an Dharma. This is why Bodhidharma faced the wall to show to others how to cut off all views (arising from the mind).

Hence the saying, 'Forgetfulness leads to the Buddha-path whereas discrimination drives to the demon-state.' Your self-nature is neither lost when you are deluded nor won when you are enlightened. For the self-natured Bhūtatathatā[59] fundamentally is neither deluded nor enlightened. The great emptiness in the ten directions basically stands for the (boundless) substance of our one-mind. Even if you move to do something you cannot get away from this great emptiness which fundamentally is neither great nor small, neither passionate nor creative, neither deluded nor enlightened, sees into everything but finds not a thing, not a man and also not a Buddha, thus wiping out space completely without leaving behind even an atom of it, which means its freedom from all reliance and attachment. That is the one-way which is

59. i.e. permanent reality underlying all phenomena.

pure and eternal, the self-mind, and the patient endurance of the uncreate (anutpattika-dharma-kṣānti). How can it be subject to debate and inference? For the real Buddha is mouthless and does not expound the Dharma, and the real listener is earless; who then hears it (for him)?

'Take good care of yourselves.'[60]

*

When a monk took leave of Ch'an master Kuei Tsung, the latter asked him, 'Where are you going?'

The monk replied, 'I am going to some other places to learn the five flavoured Ch'an.'[61]

Kuei Tsung said, 'Other places teach the five flavoured Ch'an but here I have only the one flavoured Ch'an.'

The monk asked, 'What is (your) one flavoured Ch'an?'

Kuei Tsung struck the monk who said, 'Oh, I am awakened, I am awakened . . .'

Kuei Tsung ordered, 'Speak, speak!'

As the monk was about to open his mouth to answer, Kuei Tsung struck him again.

Later the monk came to Huang Po who asked, 'Where do you come from?'

The monk replied, 'From Kuei Tsung monastery.'

Huang Po asked, 'What were Kuei Tsung's words?'

The monk related the encounter he had had when taking leave of Kuei Tsung.

Huang Po then went to the main hall and related the above story to his disciples, saying, 'The great master Ma (Tsu) had 84 good followers who, when asked questions, exposed their vulgarity except Kuei Tsung who was something (uncommon)'.

*

60. Usual words spoken by a Ch'an master at the end of each meeting, which mean, 'Take good care of your mind.'

61. The 5 kinds of concentration, i.e. that of heretics, ordinary people, Hīnayāna, Mahāyāna and the Supreme Vehicle.

Huang Po was at Yen Kuan (monastery) where the (future) emperor Ta Chung[62] had been a novice. (One day) the master went to the main hall to pay reverence to the Buddha when the novice asked him, 'If one should seek neither the Buddha nor the Dharma nor the Saṅgha, what does the Venerable Sir seek in his worship here?'

The master replied, 'I am seeking neither the Buddha nor the Dharma nor the Saṅgha and am in ceaseless worship of this (state of mind).'

The novice retorted, 'What then is the worthiness of such worship?'

The master slapped the face of the novice who said, 'What an unrefined act!'

The master said, 'What is this place where you can speak of the refined and the unrefined?' and gave another slap to the novice who then ran away.

*

Master Huang Po was on a long journey on foot (to visit monasteries) when one day he arrived at Nan Ch'uan.[63]

At mealtime, he held a bowl and ascended to Nan Ch'uan's seat where he sat. When Nan Ch'uan came he saw Huang Po and asked him, 'What was the year when the Venerable Sir began to tread the Way?'

Huang Po replied, 'Before the advent of Bhīṣma-garjita-ghoṣa-svara-rāja.'[64]

Nan Ch'uan said, 'So you are a descendant of old teacher Wang.'[65]

*

62. Emperor Ta Chung of the T'ang dynasty, A.D. 847–860.

63. A mountain where Ch'an master Pu Yuan stayed after he succeeded Ma Tsu; he was called after the mountain.

64. The King with the awe-inspiring voice, the name of countless Buddhas appearing during the kalpa free from calamities.

65. Nan Chuan's lay surname. See page 124 note 10.

Thereat Huang Po descended from the seat and withdrew.[66]

*

One day Huang Po was sitting in the tea-hall when Nan Ch'uan came and asked him, 'What is the meaning of the teaching that the Buddha-nature is perceived only when samādhi and wisdom are in equilibrium?'

Huang Po replied, 'It means forsaking all attachments during the twelve hours of the day.'[67]

Nan Ch'uan asked, 'Is it not the result of the Venerable Sir's insight?'

Huang Po replied, 'I dare not say so.'[68]

Nan Ch'uan said, 'Let us put aside the cost of the sauce, but who is going to pay for your straw sandals?' At that Huang Po stopped talking.[69]

Later Kuei Shan referred to the above dialogue and asked Yang Shan,[70] 'Is it true that Huang Po failed in his trick (to entrap Nan Ch'uan)?'

Yang Shan said, 'No, one should know that Huang Po has the capability to entrap tigers.'

Kuei Shan exclaimed, 'How fast your insight is developing!'

66. Huang Po lost because he spoke of time which Nan Ch'uan wiped out, but he descended from the high seat to wipe out space and withdrew to return functioning (yung) to substance (ti).

67. In ancient China a day was divided into twelve hours, instead of 24 as at present.

68. A very polite term in Chinese which means, 'Yes, it is.'

69. Nan Ch'uan meant, 'If you talk nonsense like that your patrons will refuse to pay for your straw sandals.' Huang Po stopped speaking to return functioning to substance, which showed his realization of the mind.

70. Kuei Shan and Yang Shan were master and pupil who founded the Kuei Yang Sect. Cf *Ch'an and Zen Teaching, Second Series*, page 57. (Rider, London; Shambala, Berkeley).

One day five visiting monks came (to the monastery). One of them did not pay reverence to the master but drew a circle on the ground and stood inside it.

The master asked him, 'Do you know a good hunting-dog?'

The visitor replied, 'I come to scent the ling yang (antelope).'[71]

The master asked, 'The antelope has no smell, how do you scent it?'

The visitor said, 'I come to find its footprint.'

The master asked, 'The antelope leaves no footprint, where do you find it?'

The visitor said, 'I come to find its track.'

The master asked, 'The antelope is trackless, where do you find its track?'

The visitor said, 'If so, it must be a dead antelope.'

At that the master stopped the dialogue.[72]

The following day at the end of a meeting in the main hall, the master called the antelope-seeking-monk to come forward. As the monk came the master asked him, 'Yesterday I did not say my last word, what would you say of it?'

As the monk did not reply, the master said, 'I thought you were a true monk of our sect but you are only a monk seeking the dead meaning of words.'

*

After dismissing the community the master went to K'ai Yuan monastery at Hung Chou. One day chancellor Pei

71. Ling Yang is an antelope with big horns found in Northeast China. It is said that at night it hangs itself up in the branches of trees to avoid being caught by flesh-eating animals. Hence it cannot be found at night and so symbolizes the profound meaning of Chinese poetry which is not easy to grasp and also the living meaning of Ch'an texts which followers of other Buddhist schools cannot understand.

72. The visitor's reply means, 'If so there is no mind.' His reply is correct and the master abruptly stops the dialogue to return function to substance.

Hsiu came to the monastery where he saw pictures on the wall.

Pei Hsiu asked the abbot, 'What pictures are these?'

The abbot replied, 'Pictures of eminent monks.'

Pei Hsiu asked, 'Their pictures are here, where are these eminent monks?'

As the abbot did not reply, Pei Hsiu asked him, 'Is there a Ch'an master here?' The abbot replied, 'There is one.'

Pei Hsiu then asked to see Huang Po and when he saw the master he related his dialogue with the abbot, and asked the master the same question (about the whereabouts of the eminent monks whose pictures were on the wall).

Huang Po called, 'Pei Hsiu' and Pei Hsiu replied, 'Yes.' Huang Po asked, 'Where are you?' Upon hearing this question, Pei Hsiu immediately experienced a minor awakening (satori) and then requested the master to preach in the main hall. (The following is his sermon:)

A student of the Tao should first give up all causal studies and should develop a (dogged) determination not to seek and grasp anything. To him the hearing of the profound Dharma is like a breeze that lightly touches his ears and passes away. If he then refrains from chasing it this is his deep entry into the Tathāgata's serenity which prevents him from giving rise to an expectation of liberation from birth and death.

All past patriarchs handed down the Transmission of One-mind only and of no other Dharma, thus pointing out that mind is Buddha for a sudden leap over and above both the stages of universal enlightenment and wonderful enlightenment.[73]

Only by a strong determination not to harbour a thought differing (from this One-mind) can one aspire to be initiated into our sect. Can such a Dharma be studied on the spur of

73. For detailed explanation of these two kinds of enlightenment cf *The Śūraṅgama Sūtra* pages 172–173 (Rider, London).

the moment? And so it is said that when you think (of it) you are tied up to the thinking demon. When you do not think (of it) you are tied up to the non-thinking demon. When you are not non-thinking you are tied up to the demon who is not non-thinking. These demons do not come from without but are within your own mind.

Only the footsteps of Bodhisattvas who do not possess (the objective) supernatural powers cannot be found. If your minds habitually give rise to the view of permanence, you are heretics clinging to permanence. If you see all phenomena as empty thereby giving rise to the view of voidness you are heretics clinging to the view of annihilation. Therefore, the three worlds (of desire, form and beyond form) arise solely from the mind and all things (phenomena) come from consciousness. The above states are spoken of when addressing those heretics who hold perverse views.

The Dharmakāya is spoken of as ultimate realization when addressing Bodhisattvas of the three classes of virtuous stages and ten saintly ones.[74]

So the Buddha wipes out the two forms of delusion, the fine and subtle barriers of the known.[75] If the Buddha himself takes up this attitude, what can be said about (the so-called) universal and wonderful enlightenment?

Since everybody likes to face the light and nobody wants to confront darkness, and because everybody seeks awakening and nobody likes ignorance and kleśa (trouble), it is said that Buddhas are enlightened and that living beings are un-enlightened. If you hold on to such an interpretation you will pass hundreds of aeons and thousands of transmigrations through the six worlds of existence which will never come to an end. Why is it so? Because you have slandered the

74. The three virtuous stages are the ten practical stages of Bodhisattva wisdom, ten lines of Bodhisattva action, and ten acts of dedication. The ten saintly stages are the ten highest stages of Bodhisattva development into Buddhahood. Cf *The Śūraṅgama Sūtra* pages 167-169 and 172.

75. Both forms of delusion arise from regarding the seeming as real.

fundamental source of the self-nature of all Buddhas, which clearly reveals that Buddhas are not enlightened while living beings are not unenlightened, for the Dharma is neither enlightened nor unenlightened; that Buddhas are not strong while living beings are not weak, for the Dharma is neither strong nor weak; and that Buddhas are not wise while living beings are not unwise, for the Dharma is neither wise nor unwise.

Thus you always come forward to claim that you understand Ch'an and when you open your mouths to speak you are already stricken with (some kind of) disease, so that you speak of twigs instead of roots, of enlightenment instead of delusion, of function (yung) instead of substance (ti). (In the absolute state) there is no room for your talk and discussion, for all Dharmas, fundamentally non-existent, are also not inexistent at the moment. They are non-existent when (relevant) causes prevail and they are not inexistent when these causes cease. Their root is also non-existent, for it is unreal. And the mind also is not really mind for it is unreal; and form (rūpa) is not really form, for it is false as well. Hence it is said, 'Only when neither Dharma nor self-mind exist, can the Mind-Dharma be understood.' For Dharma is identical with that which is not-Dharma (its opposite), and that which is not-Dharma is identical with Dharma, and where there is neither Dharma nor that which is not-Dharma (its opposite) can the Mind-Dharma, in the twinkling of an eye, develop an insight which reveals all illusions and transformations thereby giving access to past Buddhas who were really non-existent; to future Buddhas who are not non-existent and are not called the future enlightened ones; and to present Buddhas the thought of whom does not stay for an instant, and as a result of which they are not called present Buddhas.

If the idea of Buddha arises do not think of him as enlightened or unenlightened and as either good or bad, and do not accept or reject him. This is like a thought arising in the twinkling of an eye, which neither a chain of a thousand (strong) rings nor a rope of a hundred thousand feet can bind. This being so how can you think of destroying or stopping it? It is quite clear to you that it is your burning consciousness, so what are you going to do to annihilate it? It is like a mirage; if you think it is near, you will not find it anywhere in the ten directions, and if you think it is distant, it is in front of you. If you want to seek it it will run from you, and if you want to avoid it it will pursue you. You will fail if you want to either grasp or reject it. It being thus we should know that the underlying nature (Dharmatā) of all things is self-so (or so of itself) and that there is no need to be sorry and anxious about it.

The highest teaching of the Three Vehicles is said to be that the preceding thought is worldly and the following one is saintly like turning the palm of a hand up and down, but according to our Ch'an sect neither the preceding thought is worldly nor is the following one holy; neither is the preceding thought a Buddha nor the following one a living being.

Hence all forms are Buddha-forms and all sounds are Buddha-sounds. When you speak of a noumenon all noumena are the same. When you see a phenomenon you see all phenomena. When you see one mind, you see all minds. When you see a Tao (or path) you see all Taos, for to you there is not a place where there is no Tao. When you see a speck of dust you see all the worlds with their mountains, rivers and great earths in the ten directions. When you see a drop of water you see the element of water in all worlds in the ten directions. When you see all dharmas (things) you see all minds.

All things being fundamentally void the mind is not non-existent. That which is not non-existent is *The Wonderful That Is* (i.e. the absolute reality).

Absolute reality is also non-existent and that which is non-existent is identical with that which exists and with absolute voidness. The Wonderful That Is (i.e. the absolute reality) being so, all worlds in the ten directions are not outside our One-mind and lands as countless as specks of dust are not outside a single one of our thoughts.

This being so what can be delineated as inside and outside? It is like the nature of honey which is sweet and is such that all kinds of honey are equally sweet, for we cannot say that one (kind of) honey is sweet whereas the rest is bitter, which is sheer nonsense. Hence it is said that empty space is neither inside nor outside nor in the center; likewise the underlying nature of all things (Dharmatā) is so by itself.

Therefore, living beings are identical with Buddhas and Buddhas are identical with living beings, for fundamentally living beings and Buddhas, mortality and nirvāṇa, passion and passionlessness and worldlings and saints including the six worlds of existence, the four types of birth, mountains, rivers, the great earth and those who possess self-nature and those who do not possess it, are all of the *same* substance. The word *same* (in this context) is also empty (for it does not possess a nature of its own). And *is* and *is not* are also empty. All the worlds as countless as the sand grains in the Ganges are fundamentally void. If so, where are Buddhas delivering living beings and where are living beings delivered by Buddhas? Why is it so? Because the underlying nature of countless things is in the absolute state of suchness.

If you hold on to the view that things happen spontaneously you will slip into the way of heretics bent on spontaneity.[76] If you hold on to the view of the absence of ego and its object you will fall into the three classes of virtuous states and the ten saintly stages.[77]

Now how can you use feet and inches to measure empty space which clearly tells you that all phenomena are not mutually related for they are all empty by themselves? Hence wherever they manifest they are identical with reality by themselves. Because of the voidness of body this is called

76. Heretics who deny the law of causality.   77. See page 162 note 74.

Dharma-voidness[78] and because of the voidness of mind this is called mind-voidness.[79] Because of the emptiness of both body and mind this is called Dharmatā-voidness.[80] And so even if it is expressed in a thousand ways it cannot be separated from your fundamental mind.

Now as to Bodhi, Nirvāṇa, the absolute Buddha-nature, śrāvakas, pratyeka-buddhas and Bodhisattvas as preached, they are all like (yellow) leaves given as gold (coins) and the (empty) fist shown to babies to keep them from crying. But when the hand is wide open everybody sees that the fist contains nothing. Hence it is said:

> In essence there is not a thing;
> On what then can dust gather?[81]

If fundamentally there is not a thing, the three periods of time (the past, future and present) are also empty.[82] Therefore, a student of the Tao should enter directly (into the absolute state) equipped with only a sharp chopper (of wisdom); he should know this step before he can succeed (in his quest for the Tao).

Hence the great master Bodhidharma, after arriving from the West, passed through many states before he succeeded in finding only one man, the great master Hui K'o[83] to whom he secretly transmitted the mind-seal which is your fundamental mind used to seal the Dharma which in turn seals your mind. Thus both mind and Dharma are sealed, and are just the Dharma-nature (Dharmatā) in the region of reality.

78. i.e. the emptiness of things.
79. i.e. the emptiness of mind.
80. i.e. the emptiness of the underlying principle of all things.
81. The last two lines of the Sixth Patriarch's gāthā. Cf *Ch'an and Zen Teaching, Third Series*, page 24. (Rider, London; Shambala, Berkeley)
82. This wipes out both time and space to reveal the absolute state free from dualities, relativities and contraries.
83. Cf *Ch'an and Zen Teaching, Second Series*, page 50 (Rider, London; Shambala, Berkeley).

Within this Dharma-nature, who is the foreteller of future realization of Buddhahood, who is the realizer of it and who is the winner of the Dharma? It clearly tells you that Bodhi cannot be won by the body which is (essentially) formless, by the mind which is (also) formless, and by the self-nature which is the fundamental self-natured Buddha at the source. For the Buddha cannot realize further Buddhahood; formlessness cannot be more formless; voidness cannot be more empty; and the Tao cannot realize another Tao. This is because fundamentally there is nothing that can be realized; and this non-realization also cannot be won. Hence it is said that there is not a thing that can be won.

You are only taught to cognize your fundamental mind, and when you do there should be no notion of such cognition. There should also be no notion of non-cognition and of not non-cognition. He who understands such a Dharma will win it right away, and he who acquires it neither feels nor knows it. And he who does not acquire it also neither feels nor knows it. Since such a (profound) Dharma was handed down from the past how many are those who know it? Hence it is asked, 'All over the country how many are those who are unmindful of themselves?'

Now what difference is there between a student who, in spite of his six (discriminatory) sense organs gathers the idea of this (profound Dharma) while confronting a potentiality, an object, a sūtra, a doctrine, a world, the (element of) time, a name, a word, and an (insensitive) wooden puppet? If suddenly a man comes forward and abstains from interpreting every name and form, I say this man cannot be found (again) in all worlds in the ten directions, because there is not a second man (like him). Hence he is an heir to the Patriarchate and is also a genuine disciple of Śākyamuni Buddha.

Therefore, it is said that 'when the prince realizes Bodhi his heir will also withdraw from the world.[84] It is very

84. See page 106 last paragraph.

difficult to grasp the deep meaning of this but you are only taught not to seek anything, for if you seek you will miss the point. You will be like a stupid fellow who shouts on the top of a hill and, hearing an echo in the valley, rushes down but finds nothing. He then shouts again and hearing an echo on the top of the hill, he rushes up to find nothing. He will thus pass through a thousand transmigrations and ten thousand aeons to chase after his voice and its echo thereby wasting all his time in the realm of birth and death. If you only stop shouting no echoes will be heard, for Nirvāṇa is beyond hearing, knowing and sound and is without footsteps and tracks. If you can do so you will be close to the patriarchs.'

Dialogue

(A monk's) question. Please explain to me the sentence, 'It is like a royal storehouse which does not have such a chopper.'

(The master's) answer. 'The royal storehouse stands for voidness, that is the self-nature which contains all worlds in the ten directions of space. These (worlds) are not outside your mind which is also called the Bodhisattva in the empty house. If you discriminate between what *is* and *is not* and between what neither *is* nor *is not* they are all horns of the antelope which are what you search for'.[85]

Question. 'Is there a real chopper in the royal storehouse?'

Answer. 'It is also the antelope's horn.'

Question. 'If fundamentally there is no real chopper in the royal storehouse, why is it said that the heir to the prince held a real chopper from the royal storehouse and went to a foreign state? How can you say that it does not exist?'

Answer. 'The holder of the chopper who went abroad stands for the Tathāgata's messenger. If you say that the heir to the prince held the real chopper from the royal storehouse

85. See page 160 note 71.

in order to go away, that storehouse would have become empty; its nature being fundamentally void, it cannot be taken away by an alien. What do you really mean by your words? And if really there was an alien he is also the antelope's horn'.

Question. 'Mahākāśyapa received the mind-seal from the Buddha, was he a conveyor of (His) words?'

Answer. 'Yes'.

Question. 'If he was a conveyor of words, he could not part with the antelope's horn'.

Answer. 'Since Mahākāśyapa recovered his fundamental mind, he was not the antelope's horn. If he had won the Tathāgata's mind, perceived the Tathāgata's thoughts and seen the Tathāgata's physical form, he could have been the Tathāgata's messenger and was, therefore, a conveyor of His words. Hence Ānanda who was the Buddha's attendant for twenty years and saw only the Tathāgata's physical form, was scolded by Him who said, 'If you only look to the deliverance of living beings, you cannot part with the antelope's horn'.

Question. 'What about Mañjuśrī holding a sword in front of Gautama?'

Answer. 'Five hundred Bodhisattvas realized their power to know all forms of previous existences of self and others,[86] and became aware of their former karmas. *Five hundred* stands for the five aggregates that make your body. Since they saw these (five kinds of) obstructions in their former life they sought Buddhahood, Bodhi and Nirvāṇa. For this reason

86. The fourth of six supernatural powers (pañcābhijñā) which are: (1) divyacaksus, deva-vision, instantaneous view of anything anywhere in the realm of form; (2) divyaśrota, ability to hear sound anywhere; (3) paracitta-jñāna, ability to know the thoughts of all other minds; (4) pūrvanivāsānusmrti-jañāna, knowledge of all former existence of self and others; (5) rddhi-sākṣātkriyā, power to be anywhere or do anything at will; (6) āsravakṣaya-jñāna, insight into the ending of the stream of transmigration.

Mañjuśrī used the sword of discerning wisdom to kill the mind set on seeing the Buddha; hence his was called skilful killing'.

Question. 'What is this sword?'

Answer. 'It is the discerning mind.'

Question. 'If the discerning mind is the sword which kills the mind that holds the view of Buddha, it can only kill that false view; how then can the mind be cut off?'

Answer. 'Your non-discriminating wisdom should be used to cut the discriminating mind which holds views.'

Question. 'If the sword of non-discriminating wisdom is to kill the mind which sees and seeks Buddhahood, what about the (subjective) sword of wisdom which remains?'

Answer. 'If there is no (need of the) non-discriminating wisdom to kill the duality of existing and non-existing views (which does not arise), this non-discriminating wisdom is also undiscoverable.'

Question. '(What will result) if wisdom cannot kill and the sword cannot cut itself?'

Answer. 'The sword that cuts and the wisdom that kills itself are both undiscoverable. Thus both mother and child vanish in the same way.'[87]

Question. 'What is the perception of self-nature?'[88]

Answer. 'The self-nature is identical with seeing and seeing is identical with the self-nature. The self-nature cannot be used for further seeing of self-nature. Hearing is identical

87. See page 106 last paragraph.

88. Perception of self-nature (Chinese, chien hsin; Japanese, kensho): seeing the under-lying nature of self and its surroundings. Bodhidharma came from the West to teach his Chinese disciples 'to be clear about the mind in order to perceive the self-nature and realize Buddhahood.' Therefore, the first step is to be clear about the mind, and when the mind is cognized the student will see his self-nature which leads to his Bodhi or enlightenment. Some modern pundits who have acquired some knowledge of the Japanese Buddhist vocabulary, have wrongly stated that awakenings (Chinese wu; Japanese satori) to the mind come after the perception of self-nature (Chinese, chien hsin; Japanese, kensho); this is

with the self-nature and the self-nature cannot be used for further hearing the self-nature. If you presume that the self-natured seeing can hear and see its (underlying) nature you will give rise to the idea of oneness and otherness,[89] for it is clearly said, "That which is visible cannot further be (an object of) seeing."[90] Why do you place (a second) head on your own head? It is clearly said that this is like a tray on which round pearls, big and small, roll separately in all directions without knowing and hindering one another; when they start rolling they do not announce the beginning and when they cease rolling, they do not declare the end.

Therefore, the four types of birth and the six worlds of existence have never been in a condition different from the state of suchness. Moreover, living beings do not see Buddhas and Buddhas do not see living beings; realization of the four grades of Hīnayāna saintship does not see the training in the

---

like putting the cart before the horse. Readers are urged to read the Sūtra of the Sixth Patriarch who only realized satori when he chanted his first gāthā:

'In essence Bodhi has no tree
And the bright mirror has no chest.
In essence there is not a thing;
On what then can dust gather?'

The Sixth Patriarch awakened only to nothingness, which was his major satori but was still not fully enlightened. It was only when the Fifth Patriarch quoted this sentence from the Diamond Sūtra, 'One should develop a mind which does not abide anywhere' that Hui Neng perceived his self-nature and exclaimed, 'Who would have expected that the self-nature is fundamentally pure and clean, is fundamentally beyond birth and death, is fundamentally complete in itself, is fundamentally immutable and can create all things!' Cf Ch'an and Zen Teaching, Third Series, part I, The Altar-sūtra of the Sixth Patriarch. (Rider, London; Shambala, Berkeley).

89. Oneness and otherness: ekatva-anjatva, unity-cum-differentiation, one and many, monism and pluralism.

90. Mañjuśrī's reply to Vimalakīrti's words of welcome for his visit. Cf The Vimalakīrti Nirdeśa Sūtra page 50 (Shambala, Berkeley; Routledge & Kegan Paul Ltd, London).

four Hīnayāna states, and vice-versa; the three classes of virtuous states and the ten highest degrees of Bodhisattva achievements do not see supreme enlightenment and wonderful enlightenment, and vice-versa; even the element of water does not see the element of fire and vice-versa; the element of earth does not see the element of air and vice-versa; and living beings do not enter the Dharmadhātu (the physical universe) while the Buddhas do not leave it. Hence the Dharmatā (the underlying nature of all things) neither comes nor goes and is beyond subject and object. If perception is such (i.e. absolute and beyond all dualities, relativities and contraries) how can you still say, "I saw and heard (this) at a kalyāṇamitra's place where I experienced it, because he expounded it to me like the Buddhas who appear in the world to preach it to living beings?"

For this reason Mahākātyāyana was scolded by Vimalakīrti for using his mortal mind to preach immortal reality.[91] Vimalakīrti's rebuttal clearly shows that since all things are fundamentally free from ties, what need is there to untie them, and since they are basically free from pollution, what need is there to purify them? Hence it is said, "Such being the characteristics of Reality, how can it be expounded?"[92]

Now you have filled your mind with (dual conceptions of) right and wrong and purity and impurity, and after acquiring wrong knowledge and false interpretation, you go everywhere and when you meet people you try to pick up those who (you think) have acquired the mind-eye and to distinguish between strong and weak (minded) people. If so there is already a gulf as deep as that between heaven and earth; what then can be said of the perception of self-nature?'

Question. 'You have said that self-nature is perception and

91. Cf. *The Vimalakīrti Nirdeśa Sūtra* page 29 (Shambala, Berkeley; Routledge & Kegan Paul Ltd, London).

92. Cf *The Vimalakīrti Nirdeśa Sūtra* page 22. (Shambala, Berkeley; Routledge & Kegan Paul Ltd, London).

that perception is self-nature. Now if self-nature is free from obstruction and limitation, why is an object unseen when it is screened by something and why in open space are things seen when they are near and unseen if they are far away?'

Answer. 'This is because you give rise to heresy. If you say that screened objects are unseen and unscreened objects are seen because the self-nature is subject to screening, what relevance is there in your question? Moreover, the self-nature is neither that seeing nor that unseeing; and dharmas (things) are also neither that seeing and that unseeing. To him who has perceived his self-nature, where is a place which is not his fundamental nature? For this reason the six worlds of existence, the four types of birth, mountains, rivers and the great earth are all identical with the pure and clear substance of his self-nature. Hence it is said, "Seeing form (rūpa) is just seeing mind" for form and mind do not differ from each other. Because of your attachment to form you give rise to seeing, hearing, feeling and knowing but if you disengage yourself from the objects in front of you, thereby realizing (the faculty of) seeing you will slip into the two vehicles of śrāvakas and pratyeka-buddhas who have access to this seeing.

If objects in open space are seen when they are near and unseen when they are far away, this is the interpretation by heretics, for the Tao is neither within nor without and neither near nor distant. That which is near and is unseen is the (underlying) nature of all things. If you do not even see something which is near, I do not see your point when you ask about distant things which are unseen by you.'

Question. 'I do not understand all this; will you please teach me?'

Answer. 'I do not have a single thing myself and have never given a single thing to others. Since time without beginning you have been taught by others to search for agreement and understanding; is this not what happens when "both teacher and pupil are bound to suffer from the miseries inflicted by the royal law?"[93]

You should know that if you are unmoved by the second aggregate of reception in the time of a thought your body (rūpa, the first aggregate of form) becomes free from responsiveness (vedanā).

If you are unmoved by the third aggregate of conception in the time of a thought, your body becomes free from conception (sañjñā).

If you are determined to be unmoved and non-active in the presence of the fourth aggregate of discrimination, your body becomes free from differentiation (saṃskāra).

If you stop thinking and judging, your body is clearly free from consciousness, the fifth aggregate (vijñāna).

Now if you give rise to a discriminating thought you will slip into the twelve links in the chain of existence which begins with "from ignorance, disposition" and ends with "from birth, old age and death" with causes and effects alternating with one another.[94] This is why Sudhana, in search of teachers, called at 110 places but found himself searching for these twelve nidānas.[95] Finally he met Maitreya who urged him to call on Mañjuśrī.

Mañjuśrī is your fundamental Dharmakāya in delusion. If your mind is set on wandering outside in search of men of good counsel, as soon as a thought of yours arises, it ends immediately, and as soon as it ends it arises again. Hence the

93. Quote from *The Śūraṅgama Sūtra*, Chapter VIII, The Buddha's warning to his disciples against wrong practice of the Dharma. (Rider, London).

94. For detailed explanation see *Practical Buddhism* pages 7-8 (Rider, London; The Theosophical Publishing House, Wheaton, USA).

95. The fifty-five men of good counsel (kalyāṇamitras) mentioned in the chapter 'Entry into the Dharmadhātu' of the Avataṃsaka Sūtra.

Sudhana called on 55 men of good counsel for instruction and won 55 marks in his practice of the Dharmas received from them. As he made progress and advanced to higher positions he won another 55 marks, or 110 in all.

174

Buddha says, "Oh ye, bhikṣus, you are born, age, decay and die at the same time." As causes and effects succeed one another in endless succession, they are just the five rising and falling assemblages, also called the five aggregates.

If no thoughts arise, all the eighteen dhātus (six sense organs, six objects and six consciousnesses) are empty and your body is the flower and fruit of Bodhi and your mind is the spiritual wisdom, also called the mysterious observatory.

If there is a dwelling place, your body becomes a corpse, also called a ghost guarding a dead body'.

Question. 'Vimalakīrti kept silent without saying a word and Mañjuśrī praised him and said, "This is true initiation into the non-dual Dharma",[96] what does all this mean?'

Answer. 'The non-dual Dharma is your fundamental mind. Speaking and non-speaking show a duality of rise and extinction. Because speechlessness shows nothing (because it shows no discrimination) Mañjuśrī praised Vimalakīrti (for his correct interpretation of the absolute state)'.

Question. 'When Vimalakīrti did not speak was voice (sound) annihilated?'

Answer. 'Speech is identical with silence and silence is identical with speech, for both are non-dual (by nature). Hence it is said that the real (underlying) nature of sound is indestructible. Mañjuśrī's (faculty of) hearing is also indestructible. For the same reason, the Tathāgata always preaches and never stops preaching. What the Tathāgata preaches is the Dharma, and the Dharma is (His) preaching, for Dharma and preaching are not a duality. Even the two bodies of Sambhoga and Nirmāṇa, Bodhisattvas, śrāvakas, mountains, rivers, the great earth, waters, birds and groves, all preach the Dharma.[97] Hence speech preaches it and speechlessness also preaches it. Such preaching continues all the time but (in

96. Cf *The Vimalakīrti Nirdeśa Sūtra*, page 100. (Shambala, Berkeley; Routledge & Kegan, London).

97. For they are all created by the mind and should be looked into in the quest for the Dharma.

reality) no preaching actually takes place. In spite of all this, silence is the root.'

Question. 'The śrāvakas can hide their forms in the three worlds (of desire, of form and beyond form) but cannot do so (in the state of) Bodhi. Why is it so?'

Answer. 'Form is matter. The śrāvakas, by forsaking views and practice[98] are able to escape from kleśa (trouble) but cannot hide themselves in (the state of) Bodhi; hence they are caught by the king of māras (demons).[99] For during their silent meditation in the groves, they still hold on to the subtle view of Bodhi-mind (i.e. relative Nirvāṇa).'

The Bodhisattvas are determined not to accept or reject anything in the three worlds as well as in (the state of) Bodhi. They do not accept anything and are free from the influences of the seven elements (of earth, water, fire, wind, space, view and consciousness); so they cannot be found in these seven elements. They do not reject anything and are not caught by external demons.

If you hold on to something, a seal is formed to imprint the six worlds of existence and four types of birth. If you cling to the void, the imprint of emptiness appears.

You should know that when one is determined not to stamp anything this seal is space which is neither unity nor diversity, for space, though void, is fundamentally not empty and because the seal is basically non-existent. He will see Buddhas appearing in the ten directions of space like flashes of lightning.[100] To him (even) living beings that crawl and wriggle are like (shadows and) echoes, and all lands countless as specks of dust in the ten directions, are like a drop of water

98. Inverted views and practice of them.

99. The lord of heavenly demons in the sixth heaven of the realm of desire who hinders human beings in their practice of the Dharma.

According to *The Śūraṅgama Sūtra* some Bodhisattvas also appear as lords of heavenly demons to convert living beings. Cf *The Śūraṅgama Sūtra* (Rider, London).

100. Without clinging to Buddhas.

in the sea. When he hears all the very profound Dharmas, they are like illusions and transformations.[101] When the mind does not differentiate and the Dharma is beyond diversity, (you will see that) thousands of sūtras and tens of thousand of śāstras deal only with your One-mind. If you can forsake all forms you can, as the saying goes, use all expedient means diligently to solemnize your One-mind.'

Question. 'What is the meaning of the sentence, "In a past life my body was mutilated by Kalirāja . . ."'[102]

Answer. 'The immortal seer (Kṣāntyrṣi)[103] is your mind and Kalirāja is craving. The inability to keep the royal position is (caused by) the desire of gain. This is like students who nowadays, instead of accumulating merits (derived from the practice of morality and discipline) want to follow what they see (around them); what difference is there between them and Kalirāja? For seeing form injures the seer's eyes, hearing sound impairs his ears, and feeling and knowing are also harmful and are called the dismemberment of body.'

Question. 'If the seer could abide in his patient endurance there should be no dismemberment, for it is not possible to have one mind which can endure and at the same time another mind which cannot endure.'

Answer. 'Your view of the non-create (the absolute) and your interpretation of patient endurance and of non-seeking, are all harmful.'

Question. 'When the seer was mutilated, did he feel pain? Further, if there was no (ego) to feel the pain, who suffered the torture?'

Answer. 'If you do not feel pain, what do you search for by rearing your head?'

101. Which are not worth his attachment.

102. Quote from The Diamond Sūtra. Cf *Ch'an and Zen Teaching, First Series*, page 182 (Rider, London; Shambala, Berkeley).

103. The immortal seer was Śākyamuni Buddha who, in former life, suffered mutilation to convert Kalirāja. Cf *Ch'an and Zen Teaching, First Series*, page 182 note 4 (Rider, London; Shambala, Berkeley).

Question. 'When Dīpamkara Buddha foretold (Śākyam-uni's) coming enlightenment, did he mean it would occur in or after 500 years?'

Answer. 'There was no prediction of enlightenment in 500 years for enlightenment implies the non-relaxation of your determination neither to reject samsāra nor to accept Bodhi. You have only to realize the unreality of the world for which there is no prediction either during or after 500 years.'

Question. 'Does not this mean that awakening to the non-existence of the three periods of time (the past, future and present) has been achieved.'

Answer. 'There is not a thing which can be achieved.'

Question. 'Why is it repeatedly said that passing through these 500 years requires an extremely long time?'

Answer. 'These 500 years were an extremely long time because Śākyamuni was still a seer but when Dīpamkara Buddha foretold his coming enlightenment, there was not the least Dharma which could be won.'

Question. 'The sūtra says:

'Which helps me to root out wrong thoughts that have been held for untold aeons
And teaches me how to realize Dharmakāya in an instant.'[104]
What is the meaning of these two lines?'

Answer. 'If three endless aeons[105] were passed in the practice of the Dharma nothing would be achieved, but if in a kṣaṇa[106] the Dharmakāya is won thereby achieving an insight into the self-nature, this is still the ultimate stage according to the Three Vehicles. Why is it so? Because of the (subjective) seeing into the (objective) Dharmakāya which still belongs to the partial revelation of the Truth.'

104. Quote from Ānanda's gāthā. Cf *The Śūrangama Sūtra* page 82 (Rider, London).

105. According to the teaching three endless aeons are required to 1, hear the Dharma, 2, practise it and 3, realize it.

106. Kṣaṇa: the shortest measure of time; 60 kṣaṇa equal one finger-snap, 90 a thought, 4,500 a minute.

Question. 'Does he who suddenly perceives the Dharma understand the aim of the Patriarch ('s Transmission)?[107]'

Answer. 'The Patriarch's mind is beyond the great emptiness (i.e. immeasurable).'

Question. 'Does it have limits?'

Answer. 'Limits and limitlessness pertain to relativity as regards measurement. For the Patriarch said, "It is neither measurable nor immeasurable, and neither not measurable nor not immeasurable, thus wiping out all relativities. Nowadays you students are still unable to leap over the teaching in the Three Vehicles; how can you be called Ch'an masters? You are taught clearly that the Transmission forbids loose talk which only creates heresy. This is like drinking water which the drinker alone knows whether it is cold or warm. Just do not stray from the one uniform act (of body, mouth and mind) and from the one resting place (in the absolute) for a kṣaṇa in which no differentiating thoughts arise. If you cannot do this, it will be impossible for you to escape from the wheel of Saṁsāra."'

Question. 'The Buddhakāya is transcendental (wu wei) and does not fall into fate and destiny; why then were there 8 bushels and 4 pecks of relics in his (the Buddha's) body?'

Answer. 'If you hold such a view the relics you see are false and are not real.'

Question. 'Do the relics exist fundamentally or do they come from merits?'

Answer. 'They neither exist fundamentally nor result from merits.'

Question. 'If they neither exist fundamentally nor result from merits, why can the Tathāgata's bones, which were subliminated and brought to perfection, be preserved until this day?'

The master scolded the questioner, saying: 'If you hold on

107. This refers to the aim of Bodhidharma who came from India to transmit the Mind-Dharma to his Chinese disciples.

to such a view and interpretation, how can you be called a Ch'an practiser? Do you see bones in the great emptiness? The minds of the Buddhas are like the great emptiness; where can you search for bones?'

Question. 'Then what are the relics we now see?'

Answer. 'They are created by your wrong thinking mind.'

Question. 'Do you have relics? Please show them to us.'

Answer. 'Real relics are not easily seen. If you (can) use your ten fingers to pulverize Mount Sumeru, then you will see real relics.'[108]

*

(One day the master said to the assembly), when inquiring into Ch'an and studying the Tao, one should keep from developing a mind wherever one may happen to be, and all consideration should be confined to unmindfulness which results in the prosperity of the Way of the Buddhas, for discrimination helps the growth of the army of demons. The ultimate end is that not a Dharma as tiny as a hair can be gained.

Question (by a monk). 'To whom did the Patriarch (Bodhidharma) transmit the Dharma?'

Answer (by the master). 'No Dharma was transmitted to anybody.'

Question. 'What did the second Patriarch (Hui K'o) mean when he asked his master (Bodhidharma) to quieten his mind?'

Answer. 'If you say there was a second patriarch, this is identical to finding the mind, but since the mind could not be found, his master said, "I have quietened your mind", for if the mind could be found it would belong to the state of birth and death.'

Question. 'Did the Buddha put an end to ignorance?[109]'

Answer. 'Ignorance is where all Buddhas achieved enlightenment. Therefore, everything that arises from conditional

108. If you wipe out illusions you will see real relics.
109. The first of the twelve links in the chain of existence.

180

causation is the Bodhimaṇḍala.[110] And a speck of dust or any form that is seen is nothing but boundless absolute nature. The rising and lowering of a foot[111] does not stray from the Bodhimaṇḍala which means that nothing can be gained. I now tell you this, "When nothing is won this is sitting in the Bodhimaṇḍala".'

Question. 'Does ignorance pertain to brightness or darkness?'

Answer. 'Ignorance is neither brightness nor darkness which are two alternating states (having no independent nature of their own). Moreover, ignorance is neither bright nor dark. It is not bright now but was fundamentally bright. (The non-dual profound meaning of) the sentence, *'It is neither bright nor dark'* confuses the eyesight of men everywhere. Hence it is said that if people all over the world are (as wise as) Śāriputra and join together to exhaust their thinking and figuring they will never be able to fathom the Buddha-wisdom, for His unhindered wisdom exceeds the boundless empty space in which there is room for you to speak and discuss. (It is said that) the Buddha's boundlessness equals the great chiliocosm. Suddenly a Bodhisattva comes forward to bestride the great chiliocosm but fails to come out of Samantabhadra's pores; now what sort of ability are you going to use to learn from and imitate all this?'

Question. 'If nothing can be realized by study (and practice), why is it said:

Though all return to One nature at the source,
There are many expedient methods for the purpose?[112]

Answer. 'The first line means that the real (underlying)

110. A holy site. Cf *The Vimalakīrti Nirdeśa Sūtra* pages 38-41 and footnote 1 of page 39.
111. Raising a foot is returning function (yung) to substance (ti) and lowering it is leaving substance to perform its function.
112. Quote from Mañjuśrī's gāthā. Cf *The Śūrangama Sūtra* page 143 lines 15-16 of the gāthā (Rider, London).

nature of ignorance is the (fundamental) nature of all Buddhas. The second line means that śrāvakas see the birth and death of ignorance; pratyeka-buddhas see only the destruction of ignorance but not its birth, thereby realizing the subsidence and extinction of all rising thoughts; and the Buddhas perceive the constant birth of all living beings who are not really born and their death without their being really dead. That which is beyond birth and death is the ripening Mahāyāna-fruit. Hence it is said, "When the fruit ripens Bodhi is complete, but when the flowers are in full blossom, the (illusory) world arises." For raising a foot is (the state of) Buddha and lowering a foot is (the state of living beings.[113] It is said that the Buddha is the most honoured among two-footed beings[114], that is one foot standing for noumenon and the other for phenomenon which implies living beings, birth and death and all (external) things. Since you discard (this unimpeded interaction of noumenon and phenomenon) all your thoughts are now geared to the study of Buddahood because of your dislike of living beings which vilifies all Buddhas in the ten directions.

For this reason the Buddha (Śākyamuni) appeared in the world to teach people how to hold implements to sweep up ordure, the ordure of sophistry, that is to teach you to wipe out all concepts of study and views, and to get rid of them completely in order not to slip into sophistry. This is also called sweeping up ordure so that you will not set your mind (on anything), and if your mind stops arising you will realize great wisdom which will decisively prevent you differentiating between Buddhas and living beings. Only when differentiating ceases can you be initiated into our Ts'ao Ch'i sect.[115]

113. The term 'raising a foot' and 'lowering it' has been explained in note 111 of page 181.

114. A title of the Buddha who is most honoured among men and devas who are two-footed beings.

115. The sect founded by the Sixth Patriarch at Ts'ao Ch'i. Cf *Ch'an*

For this reason since time of old past saints said, "Less action is required for our Sect which formulates non-action as its point of departure, this is the non-differentiating One-mind into which most people dare not enter when they reach it. I do not say that no one succeeds in realizing it but that only a few people get through it, and those who so succeed, are all Buddhas."

Take good care of yourselves (i.e. of your minds).'

*

Question. What should one do to avoid slipping into gradation?

Answer. Everyday you take your meals without the idea of chewing a grain of rice, and everyday you walk without being tied up to the concept of trampling on the ground; thus you will be free from the notion of selfness and otherness. All day long although you are in the midst of activities you do not allow yourself to be deceived by them; only then can you be a sovereign being who does not see all forms. Do not cling to the three (periods of) time because the past has not gone, the present does not stay and the future will not come. So you will be at ease to sit erect in a laissez-faire attitude; only then can this be called liberation. Strive to realize this.

Of thousands and tens of thousands of disciples of our sect only three to five succeed in achieving their aim. If you do not strive now you will bring calamity on yourself later. Hence it is said, 'If you do not strive to settle all this in your present lifetime, who will endure (for you) untold miseries for endless aeons?'

and Zen Teaching, Third Series, part I, The Altar-Sūtra of the Sixth Patriarch (Rider, London: Shambala, Berkeley).

The Fifth Generation After The Patriarch Hui Neng: Ch'an Master I Hsuan, Also Called Lin Chi

THE story and teaching of Ch'an master Lin Chi having been presented in our book, *Ch'an and Zen Teaching, Second Series*, we do not propose to repeat them in the present volume and request our readers to refer to the said series.

The Sixth Generation After The Patriarch Hui Neng: Ch'an Master Hsing Hua

THE master's name was Ts'un Chiang. When he first called on Lin Chi (for instruction) the latter made him his personal attendant.

One day Lin Chi asked a new comer, 'Where have you been of late?'

The new comer replied, 'Luan Ch'eng.'

Lin Chi asked, 'I have something to ask you, may I?'

The new comer replied, 'I have just been ordained and do not know (anything).'

Lin Chi said, 'You can crush the state of T'ang but you will not easily find a man who does not know (anything);[1] go to the Ch'an meeting hall.'

Hsin Hua (who was present) asked Lin Chi, 'Did you mean to strip him (of discrimination)?'

Lin Chi retorted, 'Who is interested in stripping or in not stripping him (of discrimination)?'

Hsin Hua said, 'The Venerable Master knows only how to play with a dead bird lying on the ground but does not know how to turn words for the occasion in order to cover it up.'

Lin Chi asked, 'What would you do on the occasion?'

Hsin Hua said, 'Please just repeat what the new comer said to you.'

1. A man who is free from discrimination.

Lin Chi repeated the new comer's words. 'I have just been ordained and do not know (anything).'

Hsin Hua said, 'In fact it is my fault.'

Lin Chi said, 'Your words hide a (sharp) dagger.'

As Hsing Hua intended to speak Lin Chi struck him (with his staff).

In the evening, Lin Chi said to Hsing Hua, 'Today did my question to the new comer play with a dead bird lying on the ground or strike it right in the nest? After giving a (right) answer you were again aroused by my remark and I chased you up to the blue sky to hit you.'

Hsing Hua exclaimed, 'The jungle bandit has suffered a severe defeat.'

Thereupon, Lin Chi again struck him.[2]

*

(One day) Hsing Hua went to the main hall and, holding an incense stick in his hand, he said, 'This incense stick was originally intended to be offered to my late Dharma brother[3] San Sheng because he saw that I was too lonely and was fit to succeed Ta Chueh who, however, found me too slow.

When I was with San Sheng, I was awakened to the profound meaning of "guest and host". If I had not met the late Dharma brother Ta Chueh, I would have passed my whole life without receiving his blows that awakened me to the deep meaning of the strokes of the staff received by my late

2. When a Ch'an master hits a disciple, this does not necessarily mean that the pupil is wrong. When Hsing Hua intended to speak, he was wrong because he was about to give rise to discrimination. So Lin Chi struck him 'right in the nest' in order to 'snatch away the object but not the subject'. (Cf *Ch'an and Zen Teaching, Second Series*, page 92 (Rider, London; Shambala, Berkeley) Then Hsing Hua said that Lin Chi suffered a severe defeat, because Lin spoke of 'chasing an illusion up to the blue sky'. Lin Chi struck him again to confirm the disciple's correct interpretation.

3. Disciples of the same master are called Dharma-brothers.

master Lin Chi[4] from his master Huang Po. So I now offer
this incense stick to my late tutor Lin Chi.'

*

In the Ch'an hall, the master said to the assembly, 'Today I
will not ask you *why* and *how*. I will just invite you to make a
direct entry equipped with a single chopper,[5] and I will then
confirm your achievement.'

An elderly monk called Min Te came forward, prostrated
himself before the master, got up and gave a shout. The master
also shouted and Min Te shouted again. The master again
shouted and Min Te paid reverence to the master and returned
to the assembly.

The master said, 'If it were another person, I would have
given him thirty strokes (of the staff). In the present case, even
one stroke is not needed because old Min Te understands (the
deep meaning of) a shout not used as a shout.'[6]

*

One day the master went to the Ch'an hall and on seeing the
chief monk, said, 'I have now seen you'. The chief monk gave
a shout and the master hit the pillar once (with his staff) and
went away.

The chief monk followed the master to the abbot's room,
saying, 'Was I rude to you?' and then paid him reverence.
The master hit the ground once (with his staff). The chief
monk did not say a word.

*

4. Cf *Ch'an and Zen Teaching, Second Series*, page 84, The Lin Chi Sect.
(Rider, London; Shambala, Berkeley).

5. The four Chinese characters Tan-Tao-Chih-Ju mean lit. 'single
chopper direct entry' or 'Direct entry equipped with a single chopper'
i.e. *by means of a pure and clean mind.*

6. Cf *Ch'an and Zen Teaching, Second Series*, page 96 for detailed
explanation. (Rider, London; Shambala, Berkeley).

One day seeing a monk enter the hall to join the assembly, the master gave a shout, and the monk also shouted and walked two or three steps. The master shouted again and the monk also shouted. A little later the monk came forward and when he was near the master, the latter reached for his staff. The monk (on seeing this), shouted again. The master then said, 'What a blind fellow who still wants to be host.' As the monk intended to speak[7] the master hit him (with his staff) and continued beating him until the man left the hall.

Thereat another monk asked the master, 'Was that monk rude to you?'

The master replied, 'In spite of his use (of various devices such as) expedient (chuan), absolute (shih), shining inquiry (chao) and skilful application (yung), when I stretched out my hand twice to obstruct his path, he failed to get through. If this blind fellow is not beaten now, when shall I wait to hit him?'

The monk asked, 'What should one do when obstructions come from the four quarters and from all eight directions?'

The master replied, 'Hit the center.'

As the monk paid him reverence, the master said, 'Today as I was on the way to a vegetarian dinner in a village, a squall and heavy shower compelled me to take shelter in an ancient temple.

The monk asked, 'What topic was discussed in front of the Prolific Stūpa?'[8]

The master replied, 'One man transmits the abstract (while) tens of thousands of men transmit the concrete.'

*

7. i.e. he was about to give rise to discrimination.

8. Prolific stūpa: An elder at Rājagṛha who had 35 sons and 35 daughters, realized that if he did not cut off his affection for them, he could never escape from saṁsāra. So he forsook his attachment to them and realized the state of pratyeka-buddhahood. After his death his children erected a stūpa in his memory, hence the Prolific Stūpa which is a holy site where

(One day) the master spoke of San Sheng's dialogue with a monk who asked, 'What is the meaning of the coming from the West?' to which San Sheng replied, 'A piece of foul-smelling meat draws flies.' The master said, 'I will not say so (but answer,) The flies on a donkey with a broken backbone.'[9]

*

One day the master said in the hall, 'I have heard that San Sheng once said to the assembly, "When I see people coming, I immediately come out (to receive them), but after I have come out I do nothing for them." But I, Hsing Hua, do not say so, for when I see people coming I do not come out, but when I come out I immediately do something for them.'

Then he descended from the high seat (and left).

*

One day as the master was inspecting the main hall, he said, 'I have a pair of sacred arrows and when I meet a man of ability I will instruct him.'

A man of Tao (who was present) said, 'Venerable master, I am ready if it suits your convenience.'

The master asked, 'Do you know what a sacred arrow is?'

Thereat, the man of Tao shook out a sleeve of his robe. The master seized it with his hand and asked, 'Beside this is there something else?' As the man was about to speak, the master hit him (with his staff).

*

One day the master arrived (at the monastery of) Yun Chu and asked him, 'May I borrow (from you) an expedient device to show the grass?'[10]

---

the Buddha, after confirming Mahākāśyapa's enlightenment, shared His seat with this disciple to turn together the Wheel of the Law.

9. Meat stands for the dead meaning and donkey for the living one.

10. i.e. the mind which creates the grass.

Yun Chu could not reply to the question and remained silent in spite of the query being asked thrice. Then the master said, 'I know the Venerable Sir cannot reply to my question but I will bow thrice to pay my reverence to you.'

Many years had passed before Yun Chu went to the main hall and said to the assembly, 'Twenty years ago I could not reply to Hsing Hua's question because of my dull potentiality at the time, and also because of the strange way he posed the question to me, which prompted me not to give a wrong answer that might hinder him. But now the question is *just worth* (two characters:) "What need?" '

When a monk related Yun Chu's saying to the master, he said, 'I, Hsing Hua, would not say so and will simply say, The question is *not worth* (the two characters:) "What need?" '

Later San Sheng referring to the above story, said, 'Twenty years had elapsed before Yun Chu found the answer but now, after comparing the two (above-mentioned replies), Yun Chu has covered half a month of the journey.'[11]

*

(One day) the master saw a monk come (to the monastery) and said to him, 'Before you came here this mountain monk has already walked.'[12] The monk gave a shout, and the master said, 'Walk as you are ordered.' The monk shouted again and the master said, 'What a man of ability!' As the monk gave another shout, the master hit him (with his staff).

*

One day a monk asked the master, 'How is it when the royal journey is restricted?'

11. Half-a-month means 50% of the journey or 50% correct. Readers are urged to read carefully the above passage which is very interesting to students of the Ch'an sect.
12. i.e. I have finished my walk or my training.

The master replied, 'Five hundred (furlongs) are covered.'[13]

*

Emperor Tung Kuang (A.D. 923–926) gave the master a horse but when he first rode it the animal was frightened and fell down thus injuring one of his feet. The master then ordered the chief monk to buy a crutch for him and when it was ready he used it to walk round the monastery.

The master asked the monks, 'Do you still recognize me?'

The monks replied, 'How dare we fail to recognize you?'

The master said, 'A lame monk can speak but cannot walk.'

When he reached the Dharma-hall he ordered the karmadāna[14] to ring the bell and then spoke the same words. As no one responded to him, he threw away the crutch, sat erect and passed away.

The emperor conferred upon him the posthumous title of great master Kuang Chi (Extensive Helper) and on his stūpa the epithet of Tung Chi (Penetrating Serenity).

13. 500 here means the 5 aggregates which are the cause of restricted freedom.

14. Karmadāna: the duty distributor, second in command of a monastery.